the new guitar course

BY ALFRED d'AUBERGE AND MORTON MANUS

design / ERNIE BARTH

THE MAJOR SCALE (Review)

A scale is a succession of eight tones in alphabetical order.
All major scales are built in the same form:

**WHOLE STEP, WHOLE STEP, HALF STEP,
WHOLE STEP, WHOLE STEP, WHOLE STEP, HALF STEP.**

C MAJOR SCALE

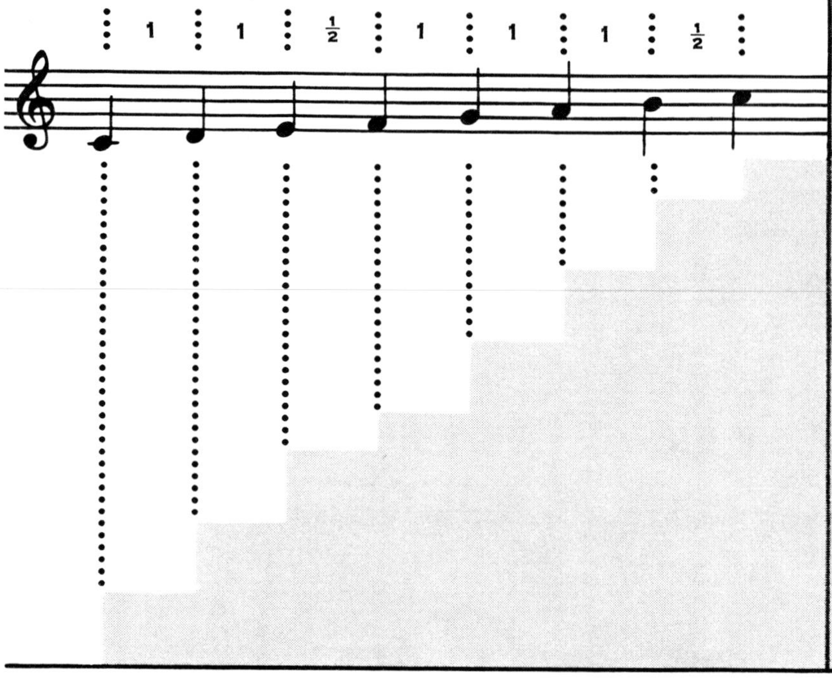

THE OCTAVE NOTE

This scale has eight notes. The highest note, having the same letter-name as the first note, is called the Octave note.

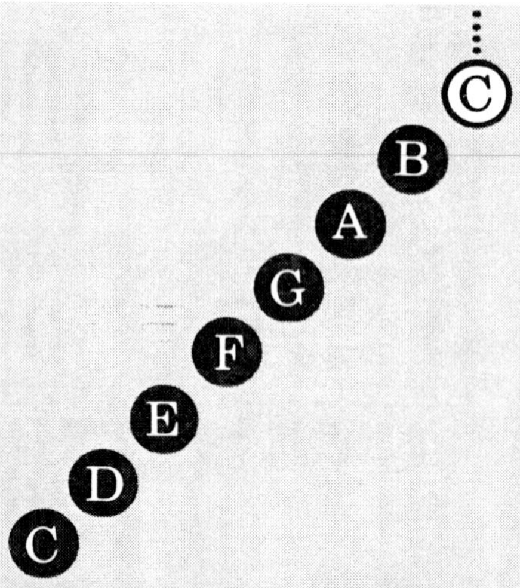

It is easier to visualize whole steps and half steps on a piano keyboard. Note there are whole steps between every natural note except E-F, and B-C.

**WHOLE STEPS
ONE KEY BETWEEN**

**HALF STEPS
NO KEY BETWEEN**

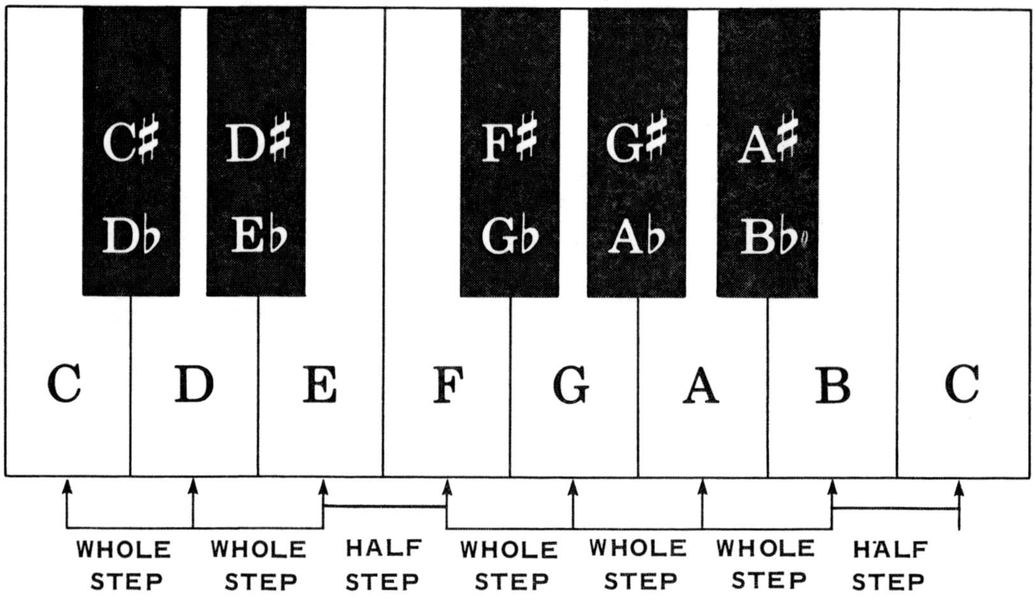

A MAJOR SCALE may be built starting on ANY NOTE, natural, sharp or flat.

THE C MAJOR SCALE

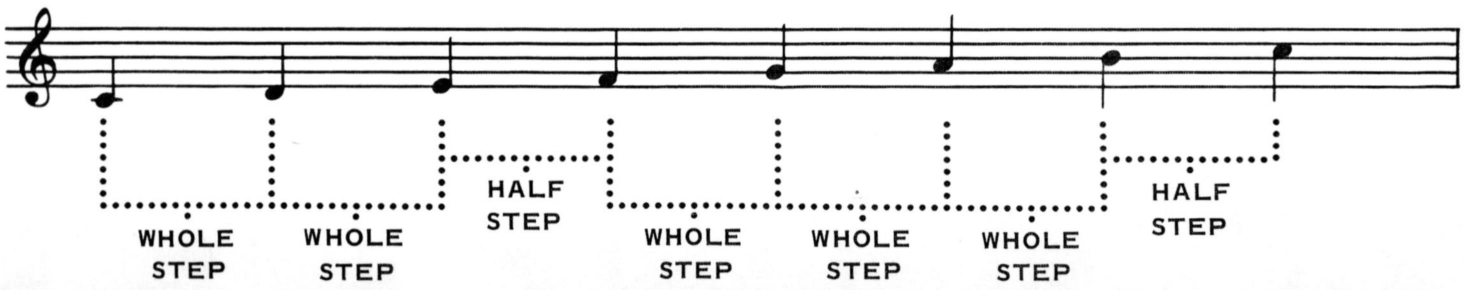

INTRODUCING THE KEY OF C MAJOR

A piece based on the C MAJOR SCALE is in the KEY OF C MAJOR. Since there are no sharps or flats in the C scale, any sharps or flats occurring in a piece in the KEY OF C MAJOR are called ACCIDENTALS.

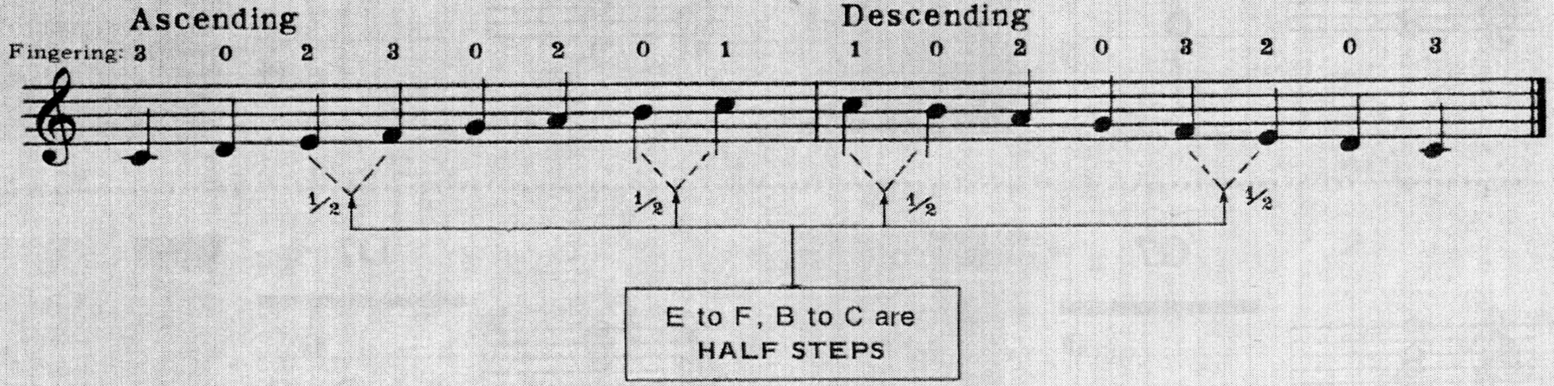

C SCALE IN CONTRARY MOTION
(Duet)

SPEED BUILDER IN C

SKIPPING ONE NOTE

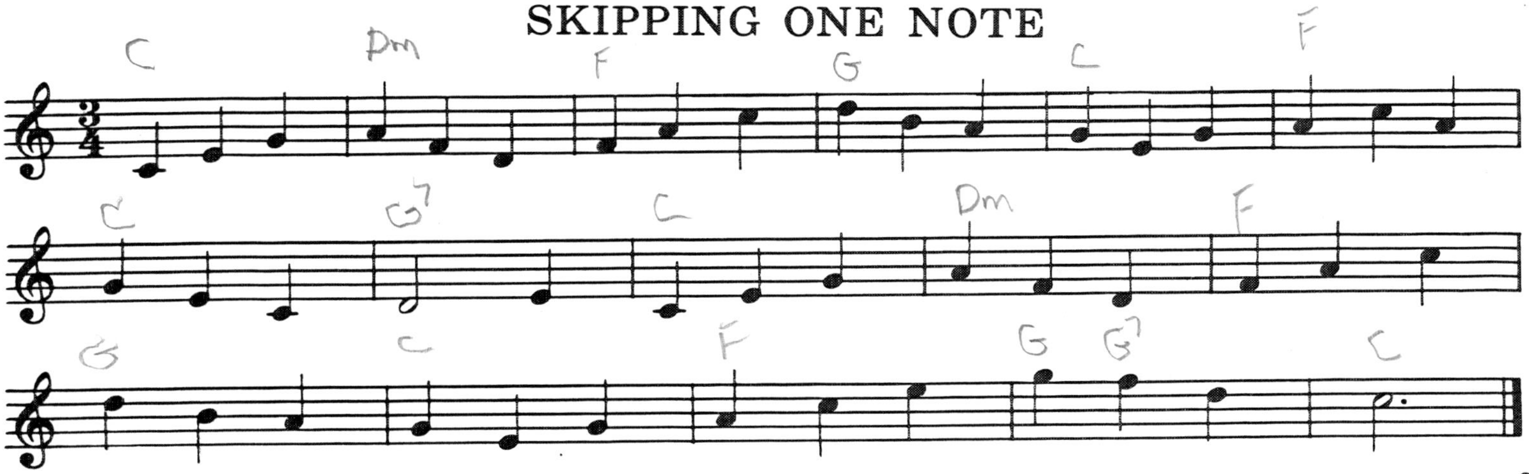

FOUR-STRING CHORD REVIEW

C

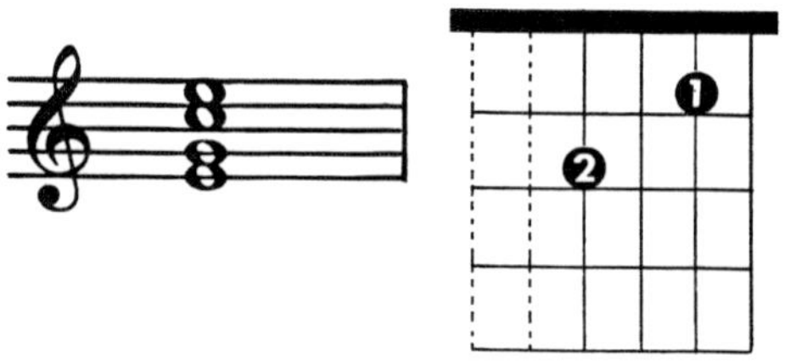

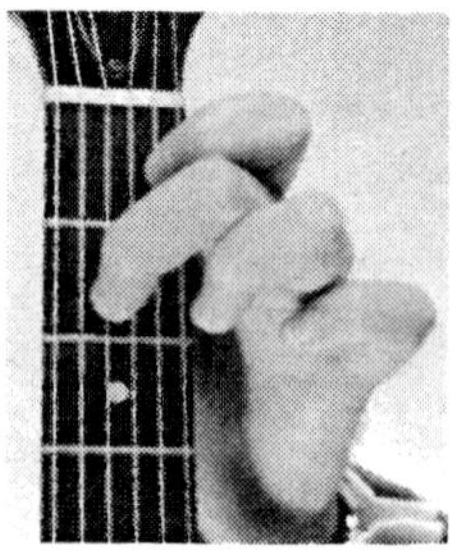

G

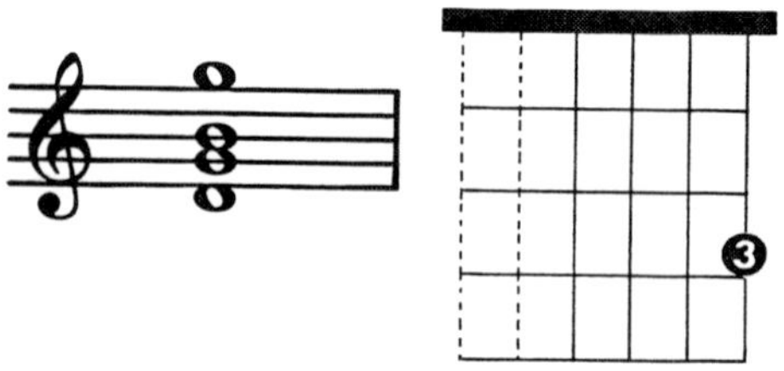

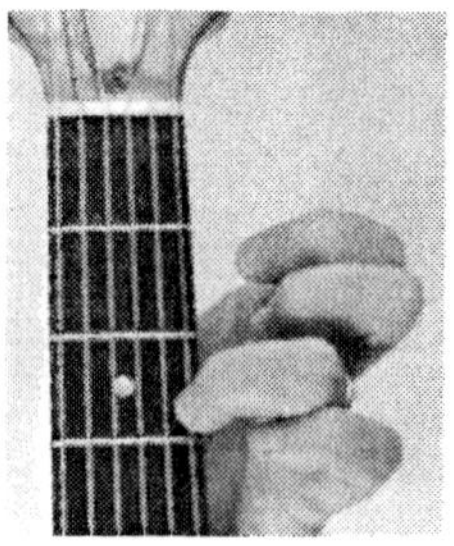

G7

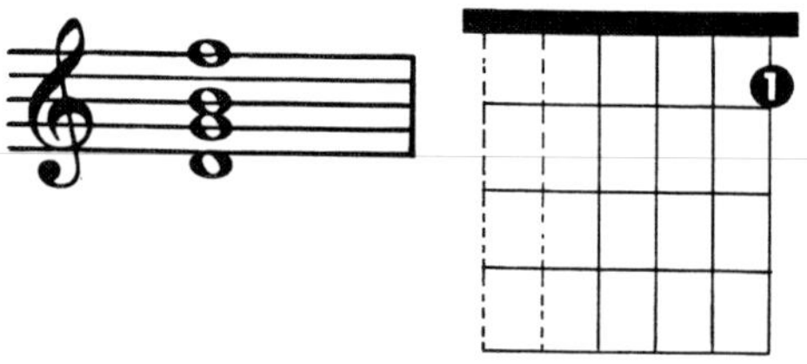

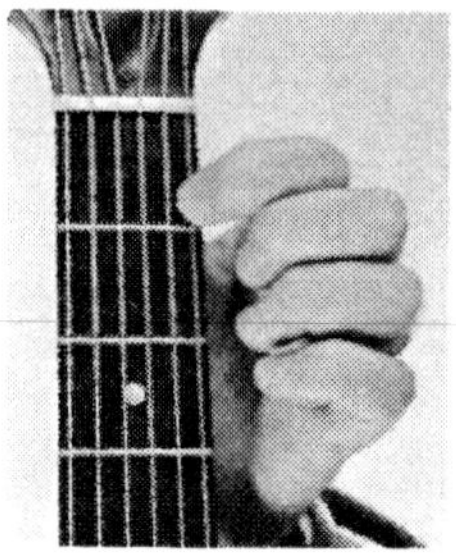

D7

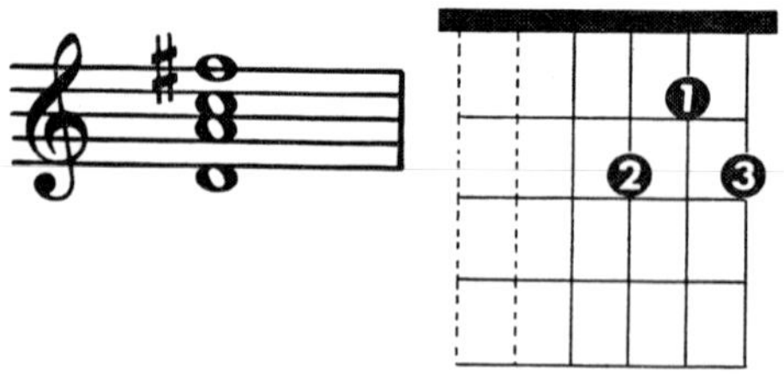

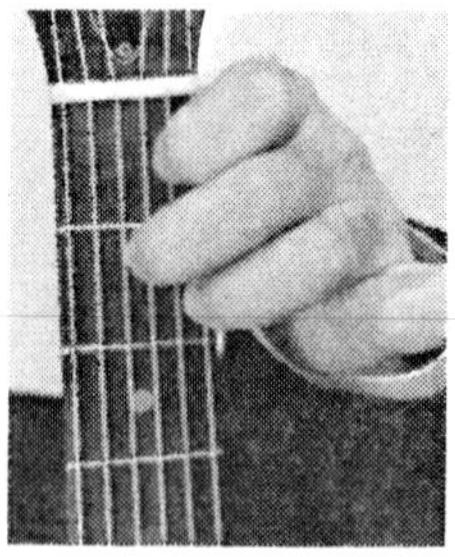

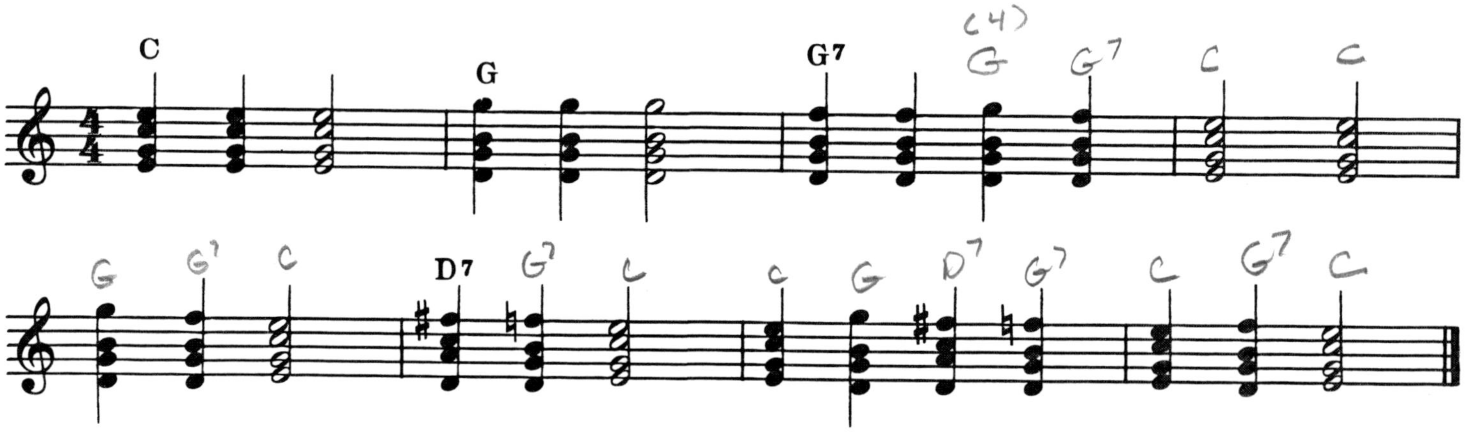

FOUR-STRING THING

Moderately Fast

ROCK 'N' RIFF

Moderate Rock Tempo

ROCK ISLAND REEL

Allegro

INTRODUCING THE KEY OF G MAJOR

G MAJOR SCALE

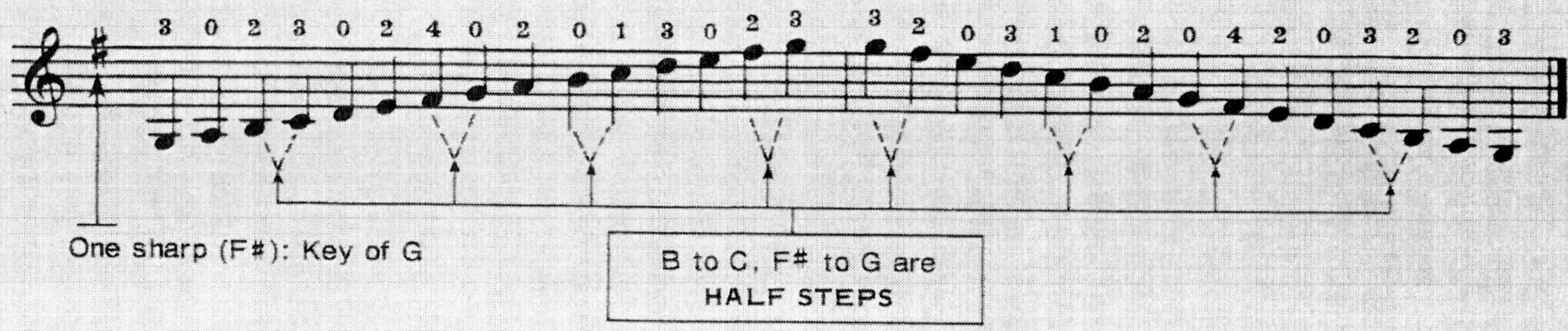

HOW TO FINGER THE F SHARPS

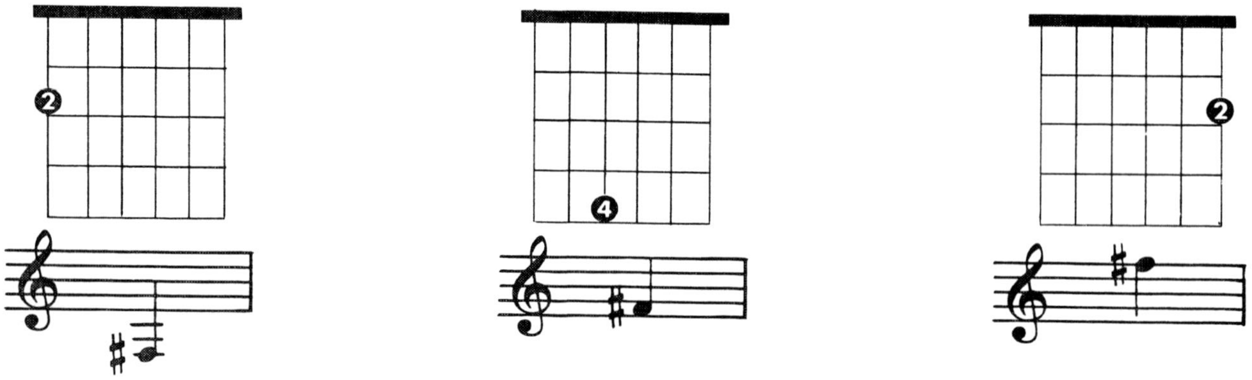

G SCALE IN CONTRARY MOTION
(Duet)

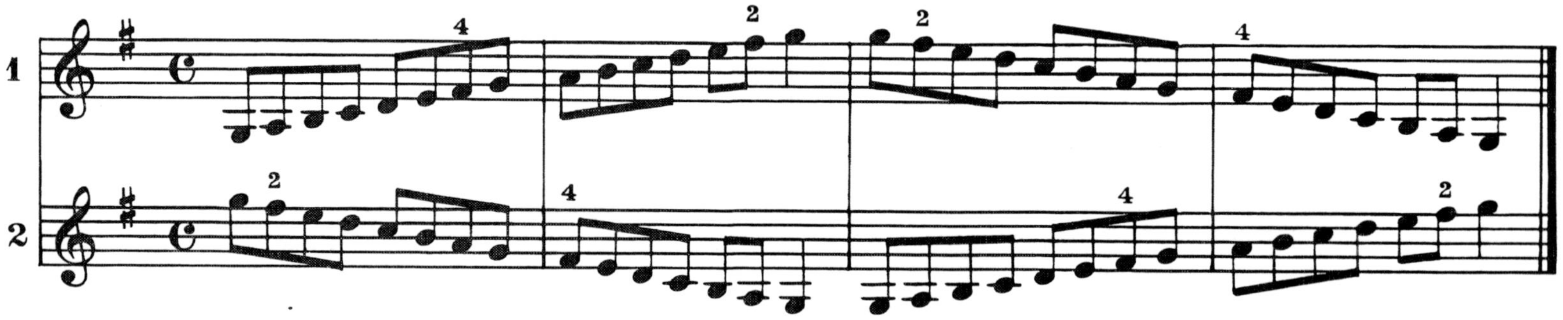

SPEED BUILDER IN G

CAN-CAN

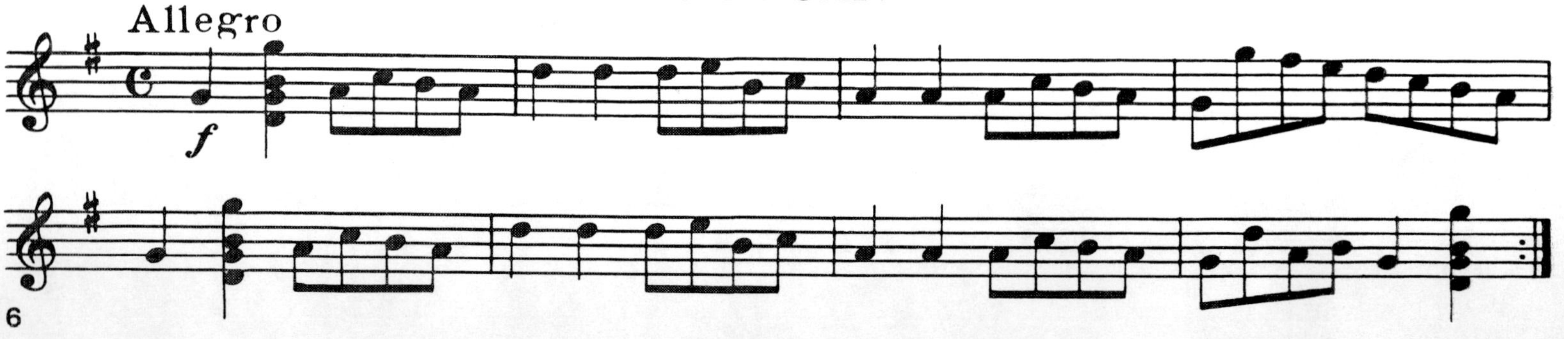

PARADE OF THE TIN SOLDIERS

(Student-Teacher Duet)*

*In all "Student-Teacher Duets," the student should learn both parts.

CORNSTALK FIDDLE
(Sing and Play)

Allegro
PLAY: G
SING: Had a lit-tle fight with my moth-er-in-law, Pushed her in-to the
C G
Ar-kan-saw. Lit-tle old la-dy, she could swim,
D7 G C
Climbed right out and pushed me in. Corn-stalk fid-dle,
G D7 G
cot-ton-tail bow, Heel and a toe and a-way we go.
G C G D7 G

ARKANSAS TRAVELER

Allegro
TEACHER ONLY:

STRAIGHT EIGHT ROCK

Allegro
TEACHER ONLY:
G / / / etc.
(Fingered like 1st measure)

THE THREE PRINCIPAL CHORDS

(THIS PAGE IS A STUDY OF MUSICAL THEORY. IT IS NOT TO BE PLAYED.)

Every key has three chords with which any melody can be satisfactorily harmonized.

They are called the three principal chords. Their technical names are TONIC, SUB-DOMINANT and DOMINANT.

The Tonic chord is built on the first note of the scale (the Tonic, or Key-Note). The fundamental construction of Tonic chords is the 1st, 3rd and 5th notes of the scale.

G SCALE

Or any other arrangement of the same notes.

G CHORD (Tonic)

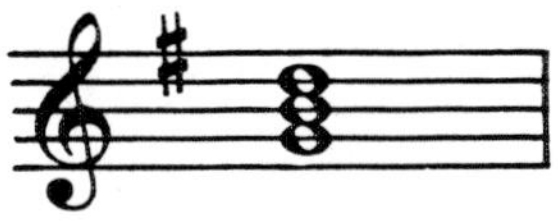

G CHORDS

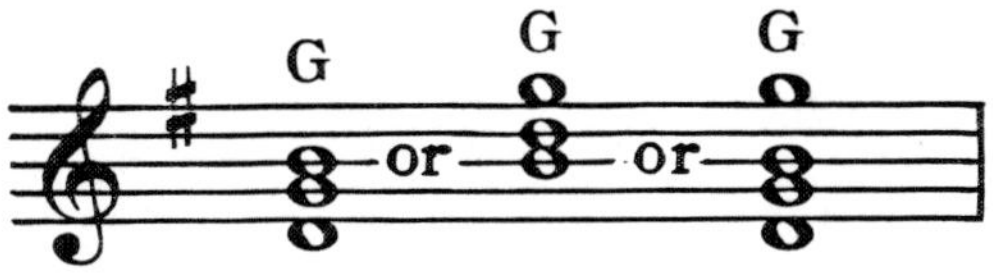

The sub-dominant chord is built on the 4th step of the scale.

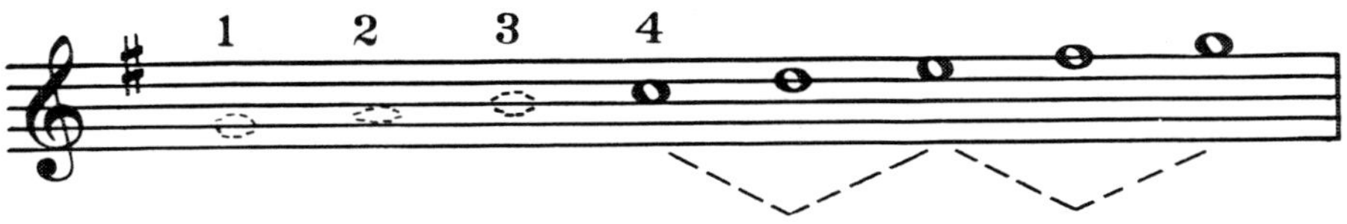

C CHORD

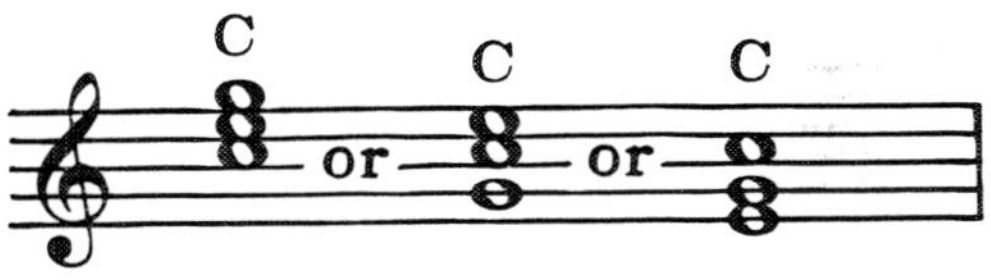

The dominant chord is built on the 5th step of the scale.

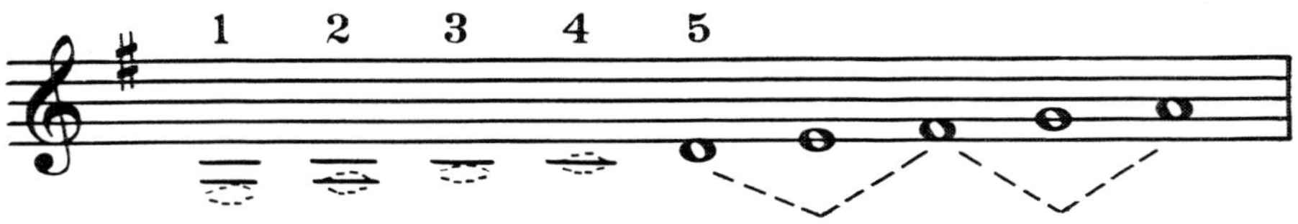

D CHORD

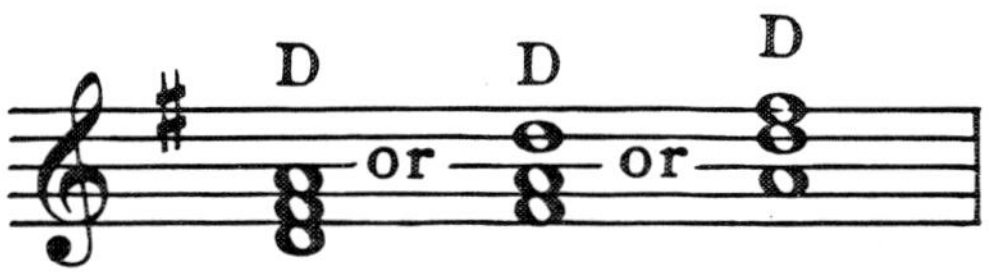

On the dominant chord, it is usual to add the 7th step of the scale; the chord is then called the dominant 7th and is marked 7 after the letter name.

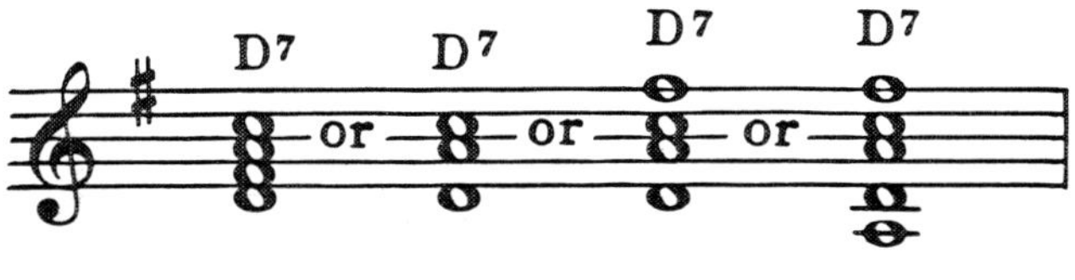

THE THREE PRINCIPAL CHORDS IN THE KEY OF G MAJOR

THE 6 STRING G CHORD

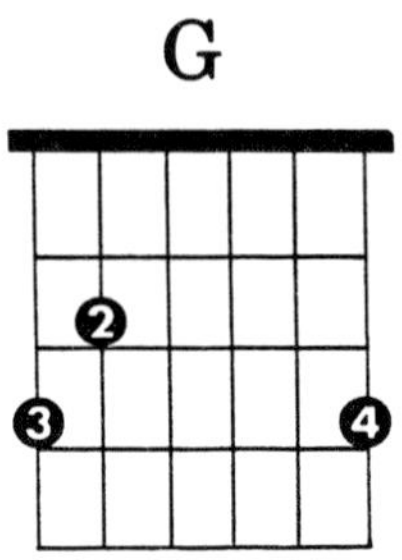

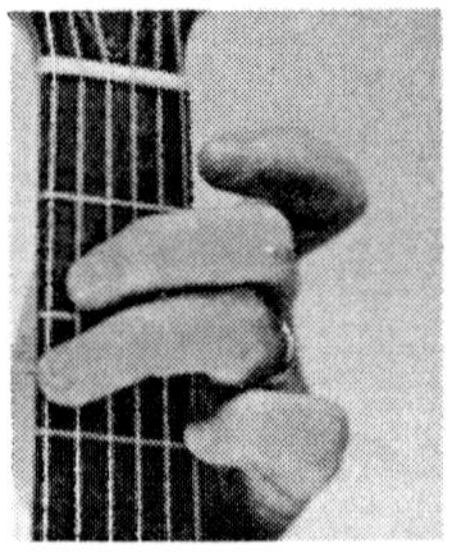

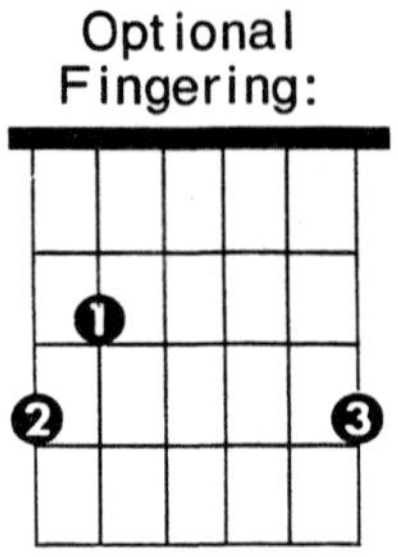

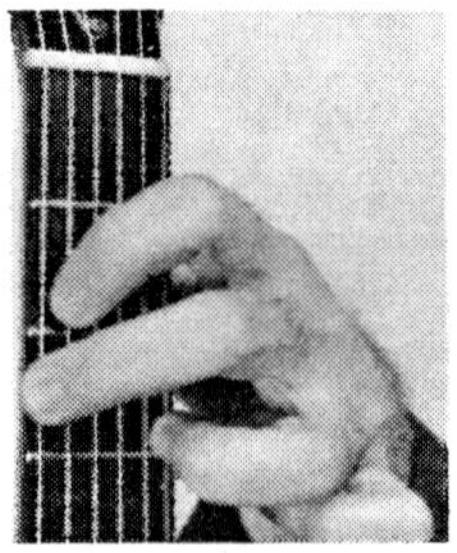

Though the 3-1-2 fingering is originally easier to use, the 4-2-3 fingering offers so many advantages when switching to other chords, it is strongly recommended the student take the extra pains to learn it.

6 STRING G CHORD:

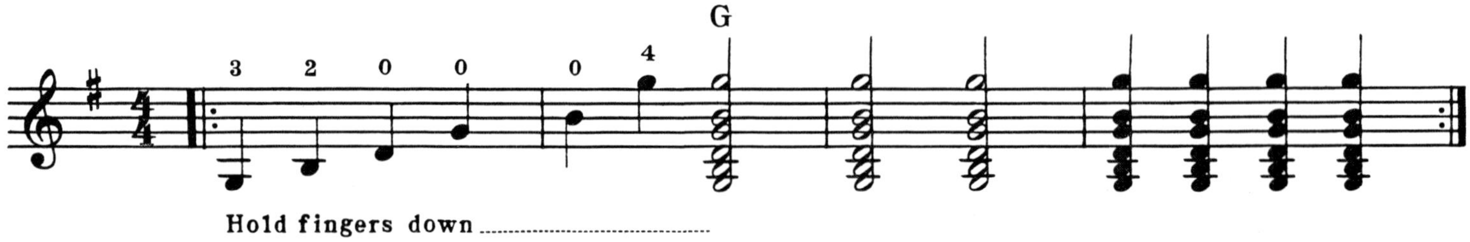

Chord Accompaniment is considerably improved by replacing the first chord of each measure with a bass note. The simplest bass note is the root (the letter-name) of the chord.

G CHORD WITH BASS NOTE:

THE 5 STRING C CHORD

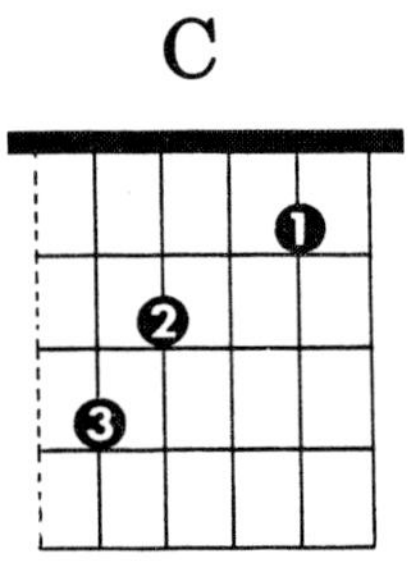

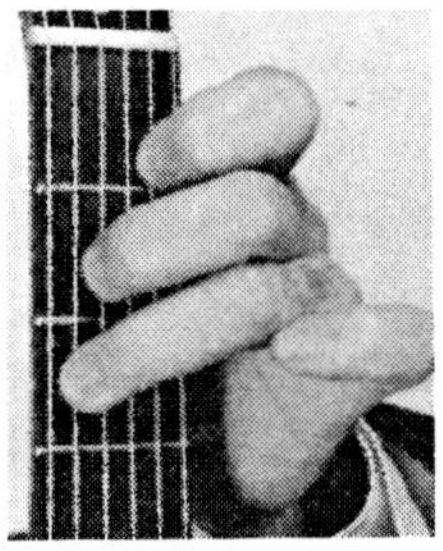

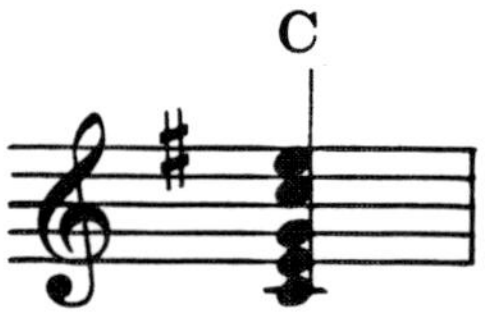

5 STRING C CHORD:

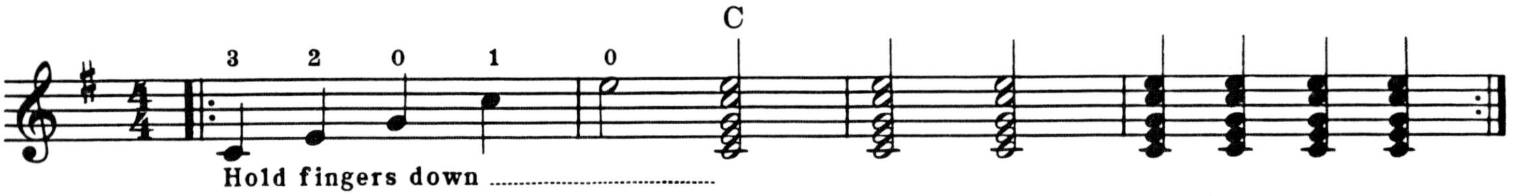

C CHORD WITH BASS NOTE:

THE 4 STRING D7 CHORD

D7

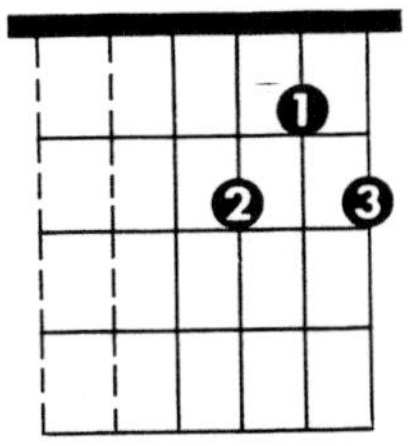

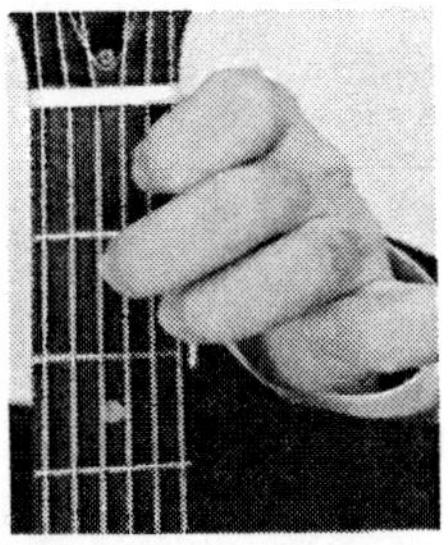

D7

0
2
1
3
D7
Hold fingers down

D7 WITH BASS NOTE:

OLD DAN TUCKER
(Sing and Play)

This piece introduces bass and chord accompaniment. Play the accompaniment while your teacher plays the solo part. Play the same accompaniment and sing the words.

Allegro
SOLO
ACCOM-PANIMENT
G
D7
I come to town the oth-er night, I heard some noise and saw a fight,
f
1
2
Watch-man was a - run-ning 'round, shout-ing "Old Dan Tuck-er's come to town."
C
Get out the way for old Dan Tuck-er, come to late to get his sup-per,
Sup-per o - ver, break-fast cook-ing, old Dan Tuck-er just stands 'round look-ing.

ALTERNATING BASS NOTES IN KEY OF G

An alternating bass note is any note except the root of the chord. Alternate bass notes are used to enrich the accompaniment when the harmony remains the same for several consecutive measures.

G

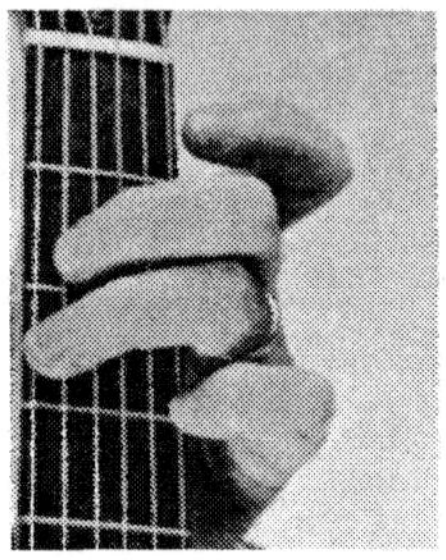

Optional Fingering:

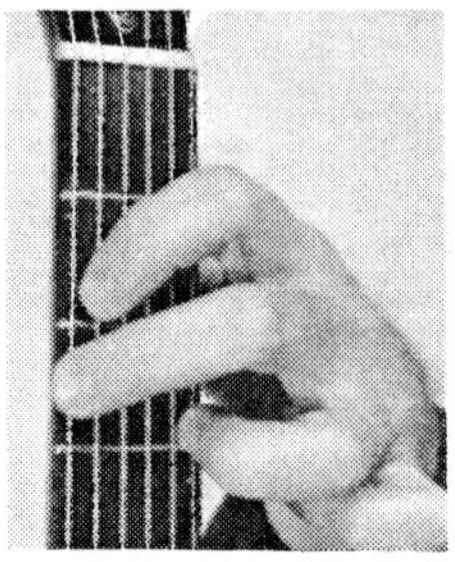

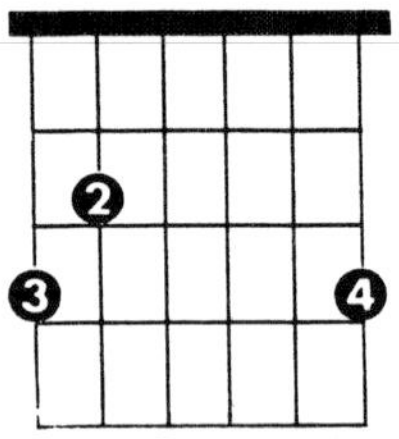

G D–Alternate Bass Note
Bass Note

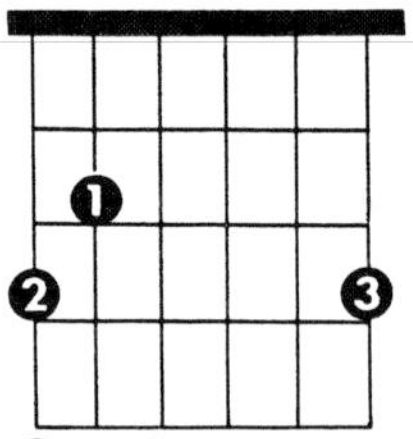

G D–Alternate Bass Note
Bass Note

C

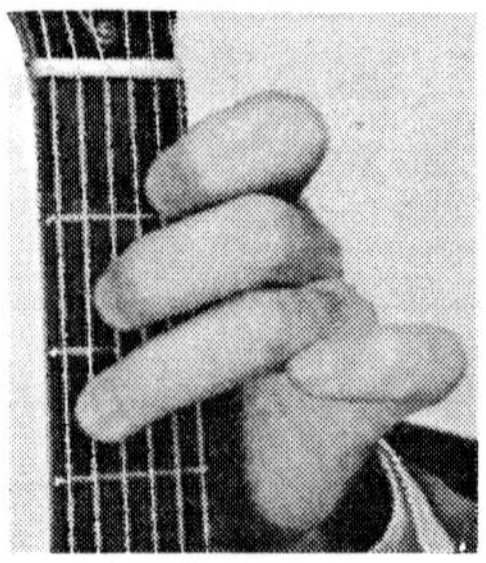

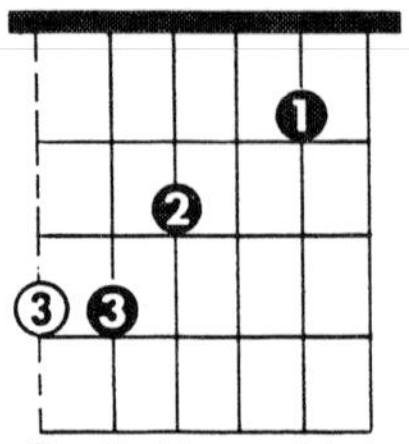

G C–Bass Note
Alternate Bass Note

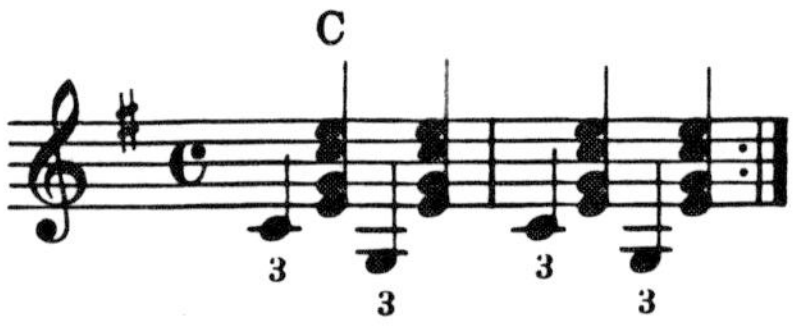

D7

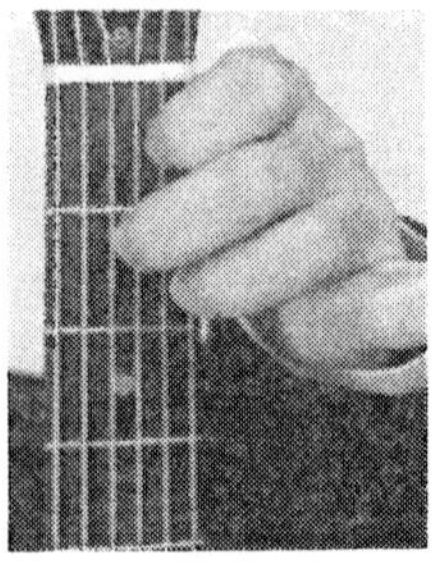

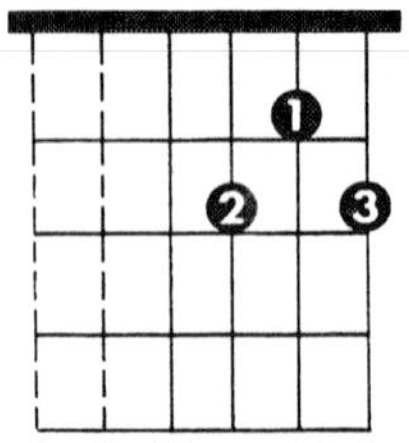

A D–Bass Note
Alternate Bass Note

ACCOMPANIMENT IN G MAJOR

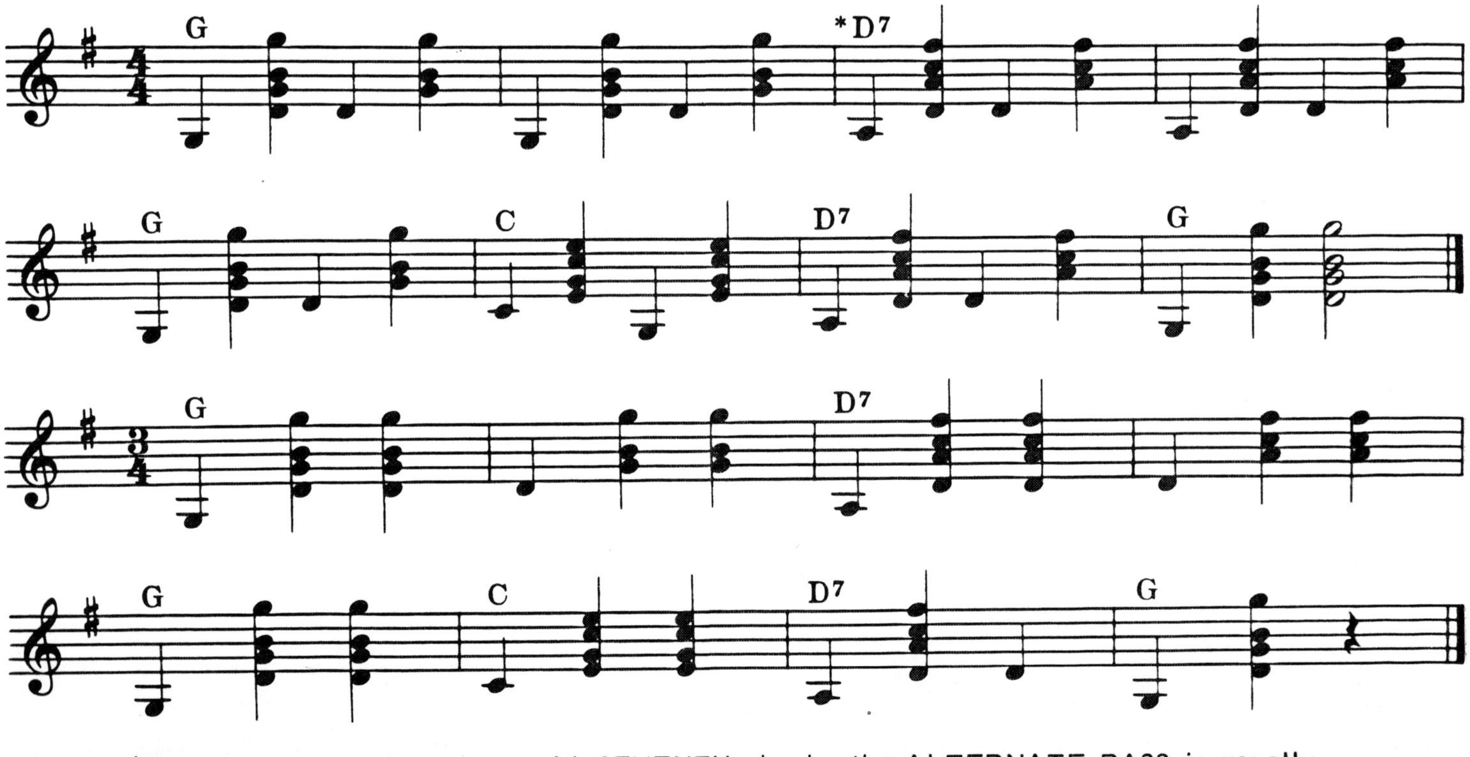

*When alternating the basses with SEVENTH chords, the ALTERNATE BASS is usually sounded first!

OH, HOW HE LIED

(Alternating basses in $\frac{3}{4}$ time)

Allegro
SOLO
ACCOM-PANIMENT
mf
G
D7
C
He sat down be - side her and smoked his ci - gar, smoked his ci - gar, smoked his ci - gar, He sat down be - side her and smoked his ci - gar, smoked his ci - gar - r - r.

2. There was a young maiden
Who played a guitar,
Played a guitar,
Played a guitar,
There was a young maiden
Who played a guitar,
Played a guitar - r - r.

3. He told her he loved her
But, oh, how he lied,
Oh, how he lied,
Oh, how he lied,
He told her he loved her
But, oh, how he lied,
Oh, how he lied - ied - ied.

THE HORSES RUN AROUND

The student may add an accompaniment to this song, using bass and alternating bass notes. The chord symbols above the staff show which chords to use. The accompaniment below the first line will serve as an example. Remember to play the alternating bass first with the G7 chord. This accompaniment may be played while the melody is sung, and while the teacher plays the melody.

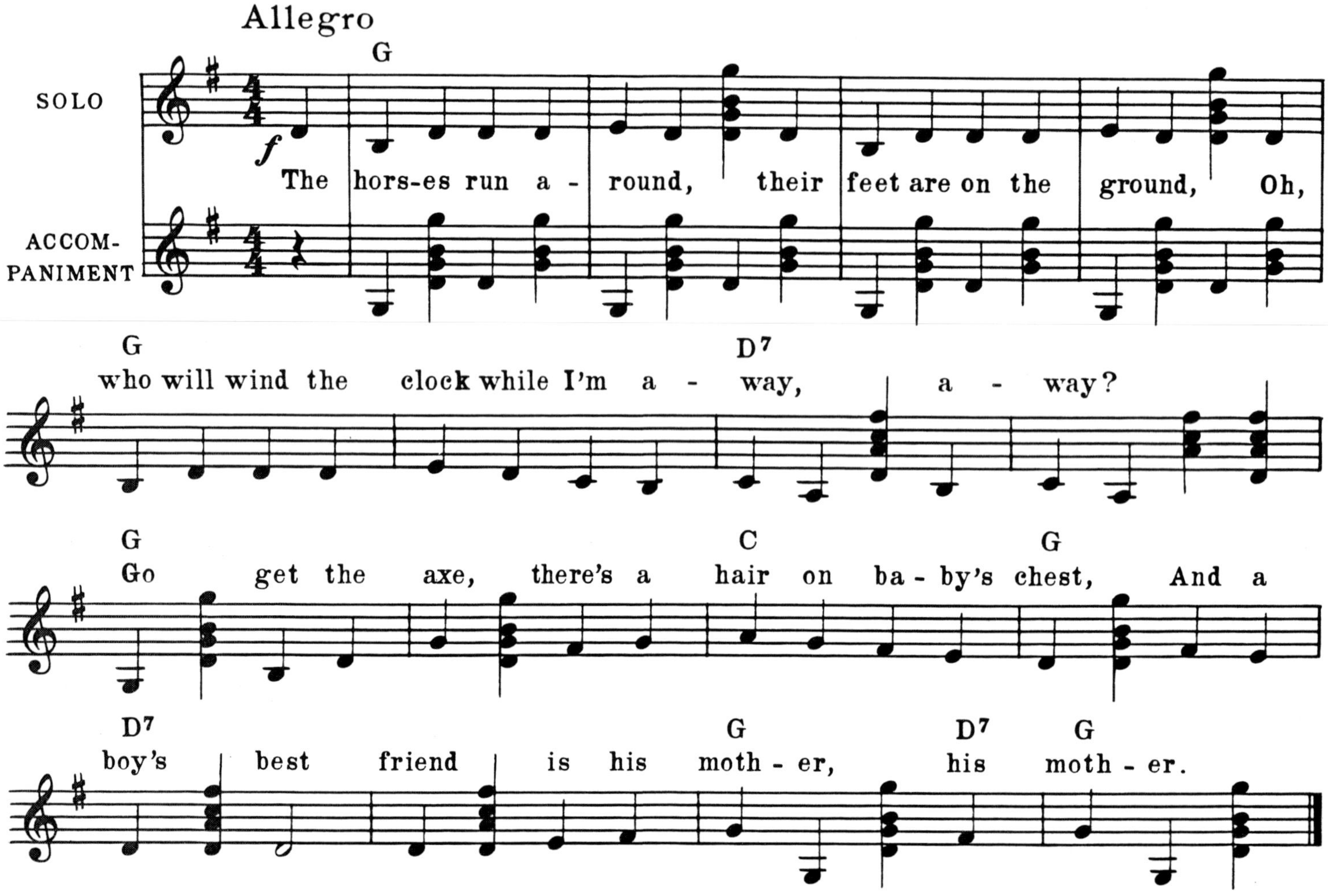
Allegro
SOLO
ACCOM-PANIMENT
G
The hors-es run a - round, their feet are on the ground, Oh,
G D7
who will wind the clock while I'm a - way, a - way?
G C G
Go get the axe, there's a hair on ba - by's chest, And a
D7 G D7 G
boy's best friend is his moth - er, his moth - er.

"DOUBLE NOTE BLUES"

This selection introduces the double notes B and D, which are played as shown in the diagram on the right.

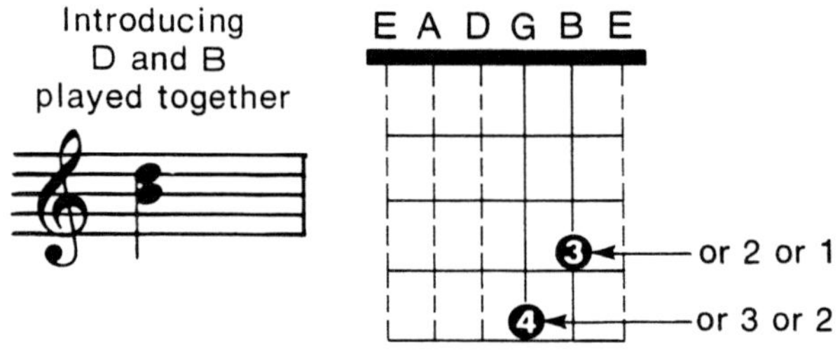
Introducing
D and B
played together
E A D G B E
or 2 or 1
or 3 or 2

Moderato
TEACHER ONLY: G / / / etc.
C7
G
D7
G

BASS SOLOS WITH CHORD ACCOMPANIMENT

When bass solos are played with chord accompaniment, the solo part is written with the stems descending, the chords with ascending stems.

This bass solo begins on the first beat and is held for three beats. The quarter rest shows that the accompaniment begins on the 2nd beat.

LOW DOWN BLUES

Moderately slow

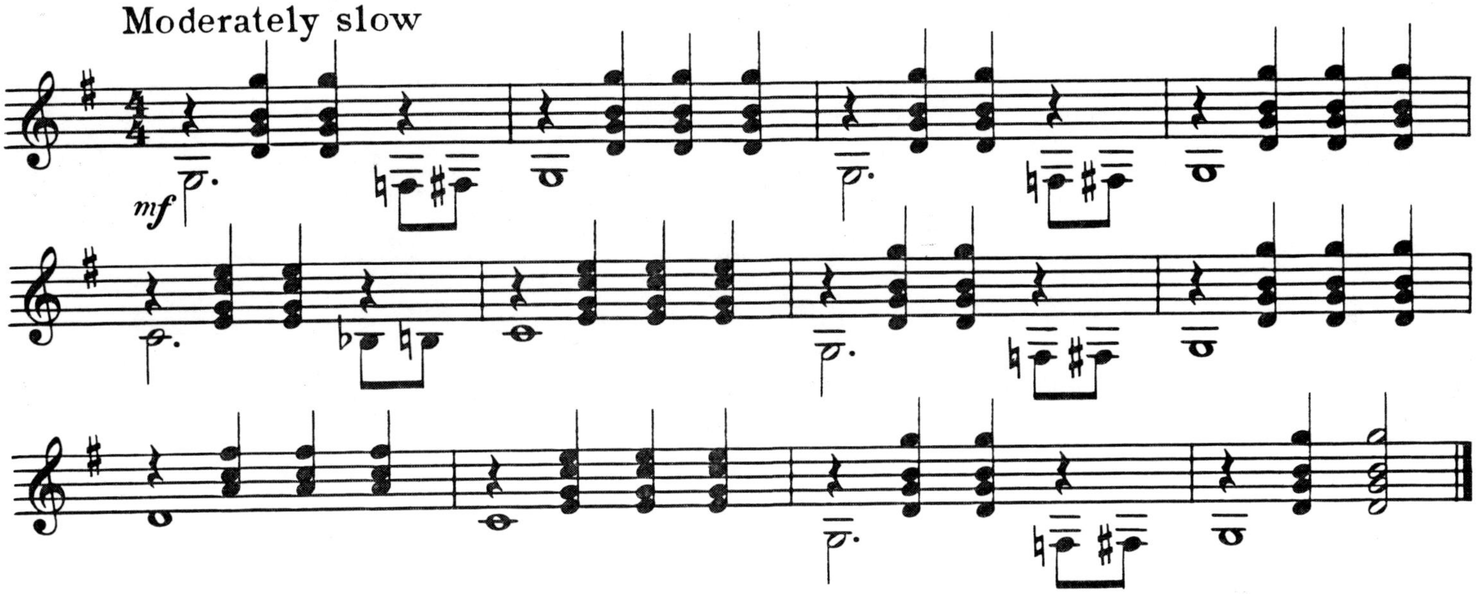

ALMA MATER

(Sing and Play)

Moderato

PLAY: G C D7 G
SING: Sing we now the joy-ous song, "Life to Al-ma Ma - ter!"
G C D7 G
Sing we now the joy-ous song, "Life to Al-ma Ma - ter!"
D7 G D7 G D7
Life to each pro - fes-sor here, Life to all our com-rades dear,
G C G D7 G C G D7 G
May they nev-er leave us, May they nev - er leave us.
(3)
(3)

INTRODUCING TRIPLETS

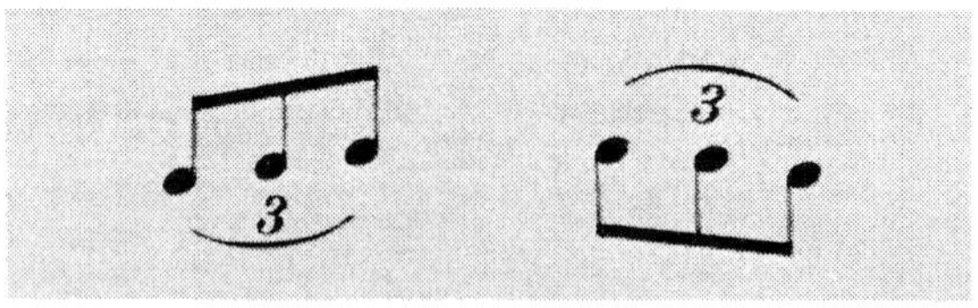

When three notes are grouped together with the figure "3" above or below the notes, the group is called a TRIPLET.

The *three* notes then have the same value as is ordinarily given to *two* of the notes.

In $\frac{3}{4}$ or $\frac{4}{4}$ time, *two* eighth notes get one count, so an eighth note TRIPLET will also get one count.

In the following exercise play the three notes of each triplet on one count.

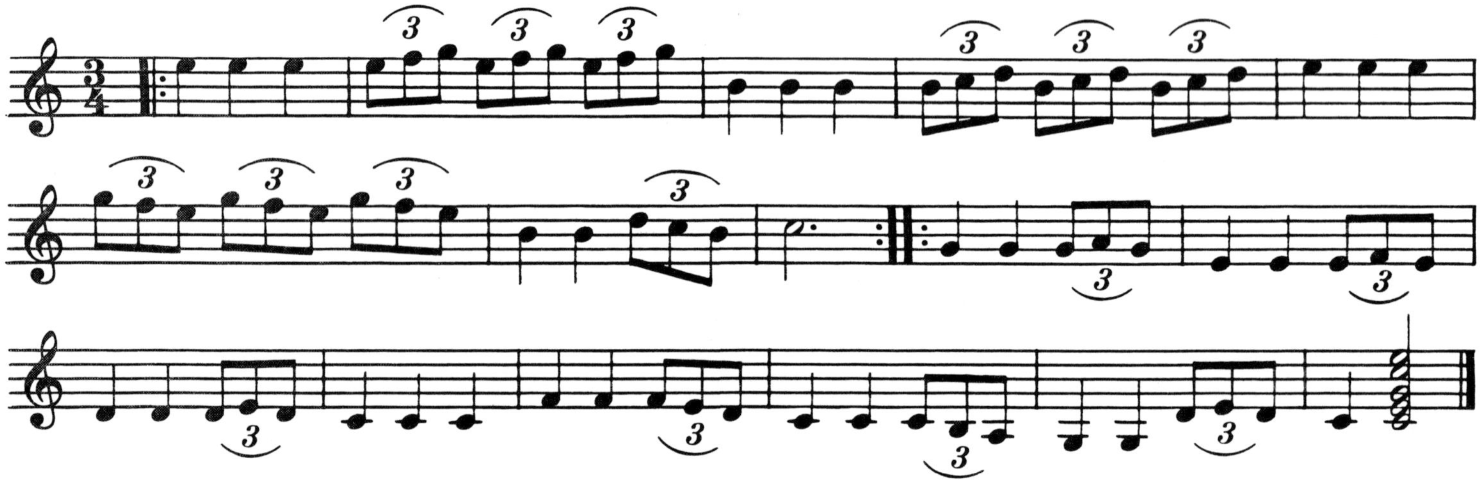

BEAUTIFUL DREAMER

Andante

TRIPLE VIBRATION

Triplets form an important part of the Rock 'n' Roll style, particularly in the slower "ballad" type of songs. Here is a typical example:

Andante

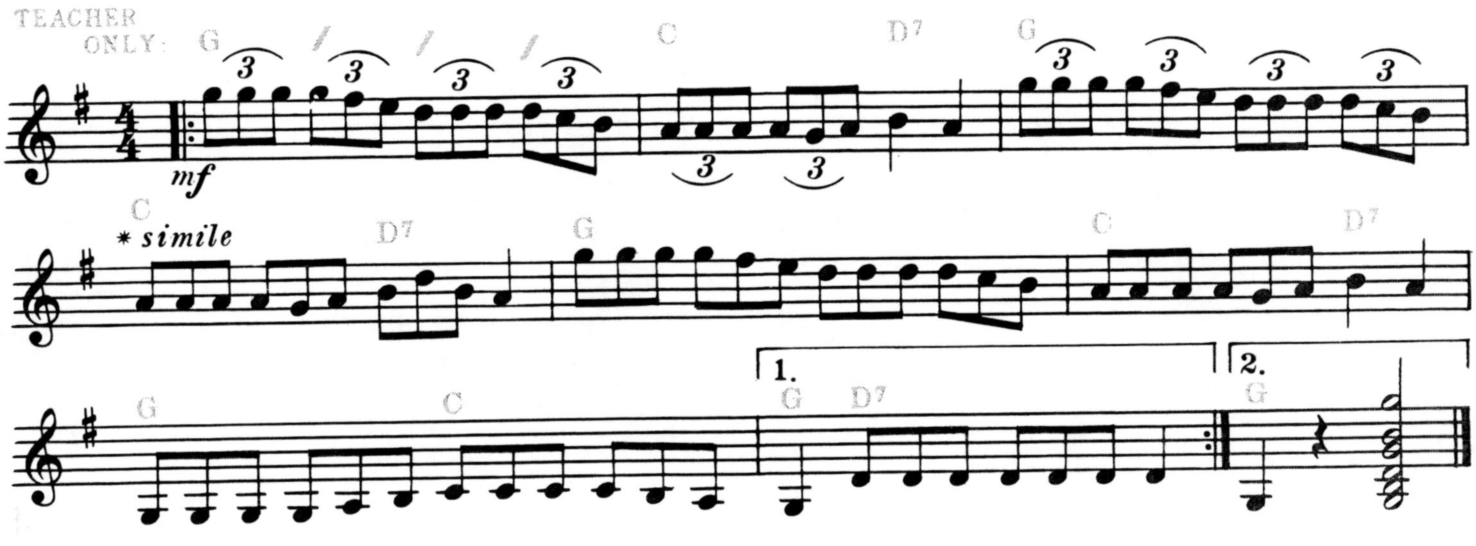

Many Rock 'n' Roll tunes (fast and slow) use the rhythm shown in the second measure of the following example. The eighth rest (𝄾) is substituted for the second eighth note of the triplet:

COUNT YOURSELF IN!

Moderately fast

**simile – continue (triplets) in the same manner.*

INTRODUCING THE MINOR KEYS

A minor scale, like the major, is a succession of eight tones in alphabetical rotation. The method of dividing these eight tones into steps and half steps establishes the mode (or style) of the music. Our Western music, as distinguished from Oriental music, has only two modes: major and minor. When the steps of the scale progress in the form:

WHOLE STEP, WHOLE STEP, HALF STEP,
WHOLE STEP, WHOLE STEP, WHOLE STEP, HALF STEP,

the scale is a Major scale and the music is in the Major Mode.

G MAJOR SCALE

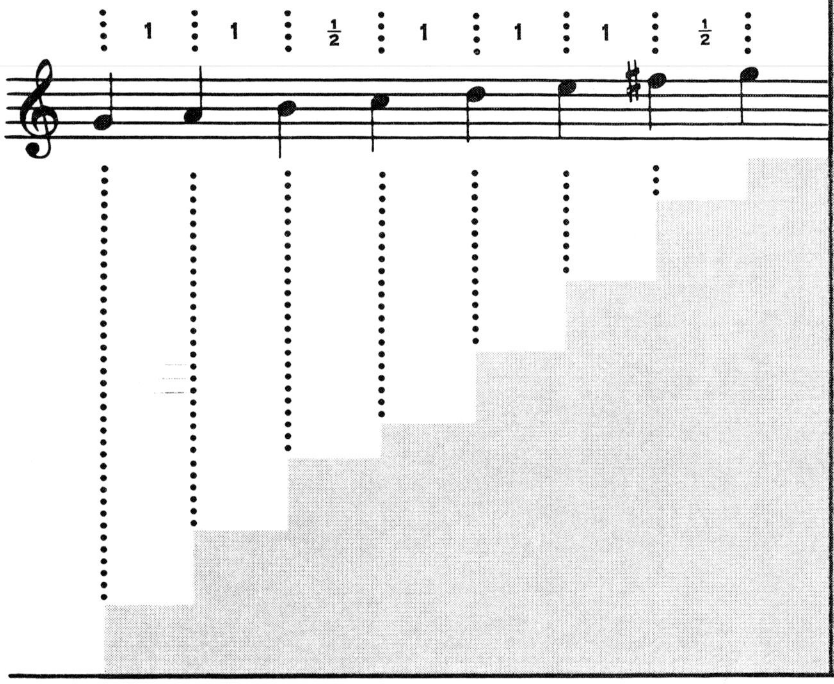

THE OCTAVE NOTE

This scale has eight notes. The highest note, having the same letter-name as the first note is called the Octave note.

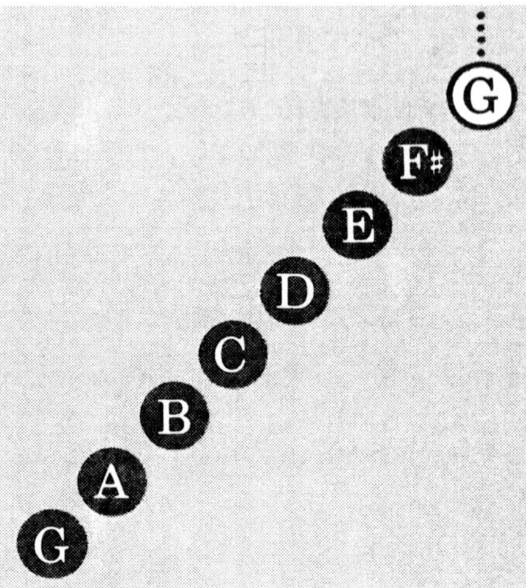

When the steps of the scale progress in the form:

WHOLE STEP, HALF STEP, WHOLE STEP,
WHOLE STEP, HALF STEP, ONE AND ONE-HALF STEP, HALF STEP,

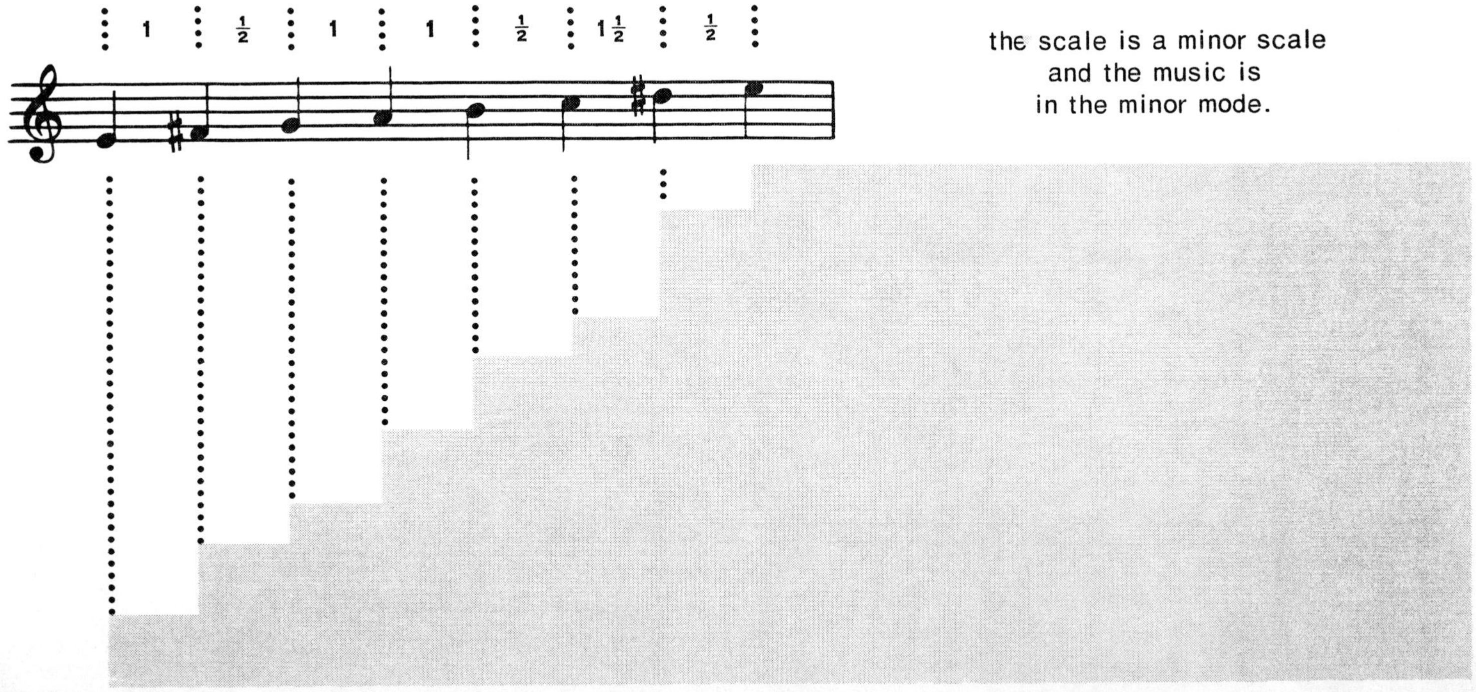

the scale is a minor scale and the music is in the minor mode.

THE KEY OF E MINOR

For every major key there is a minor key with the same key signature. E minor and G major are called RELATIVE keys because they both have the same key signature, one sharp (F#).

The relative minor scale is built on the 6th tone of the major scale.

Chords are built on the HARMONIC MINOR scale, which has its 7th tone augmented (raised a half step).

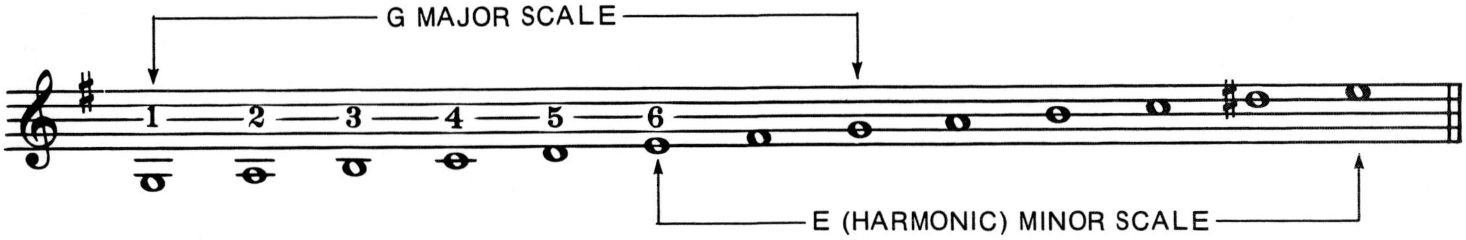

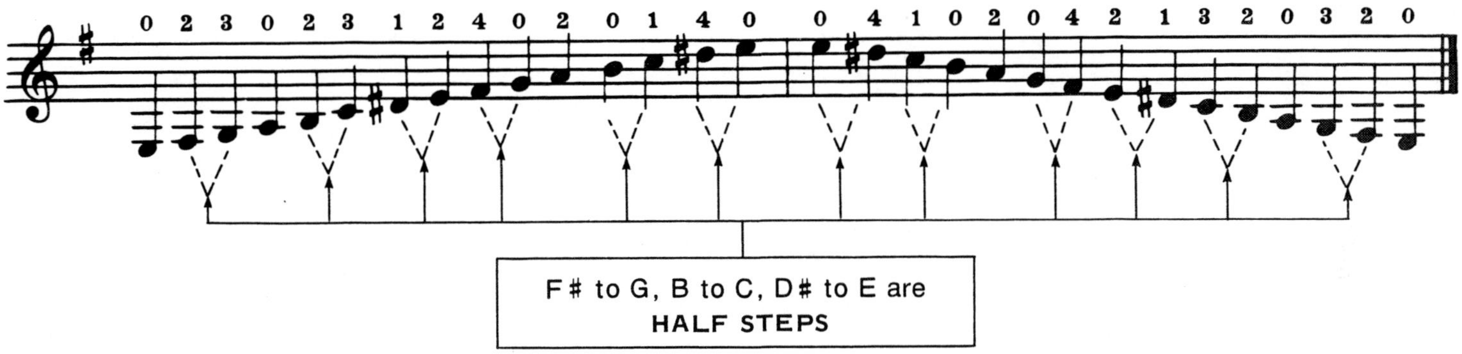

E MINOR SCALE IN CONTRARY MOTION
(Duet)

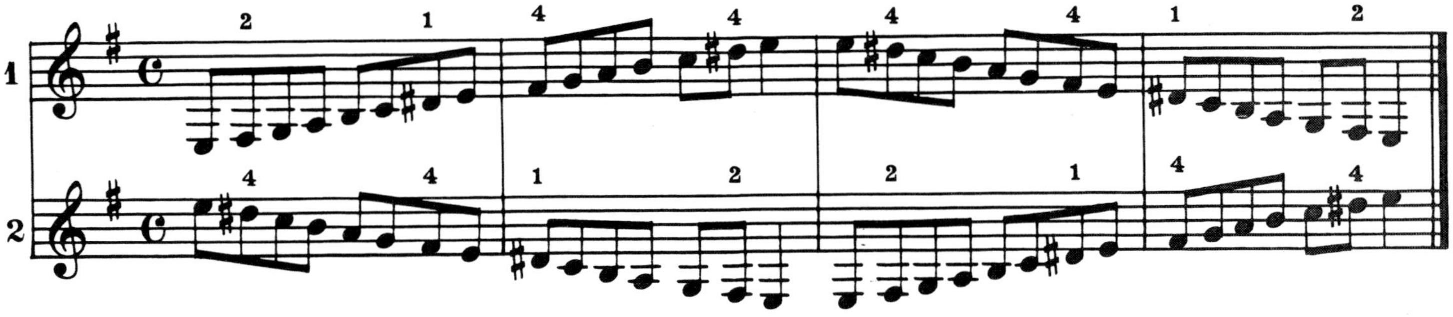

MINKA, MINKA

Andante

THE THREE PRINCIPAL CHORDS IN THE KEY OF E MINOR

Em

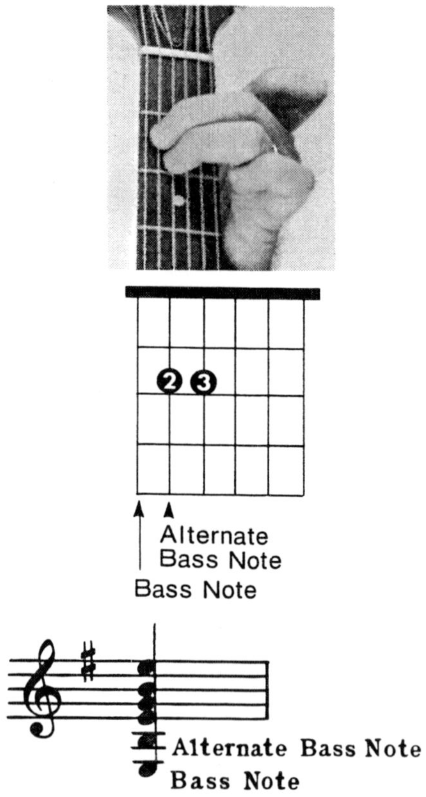

Am

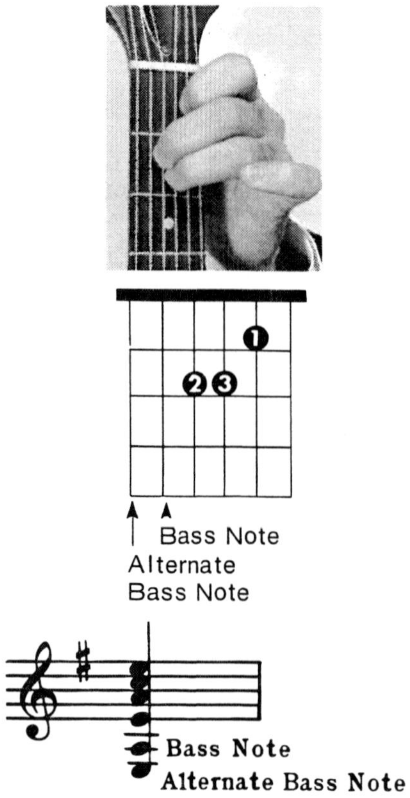

B7

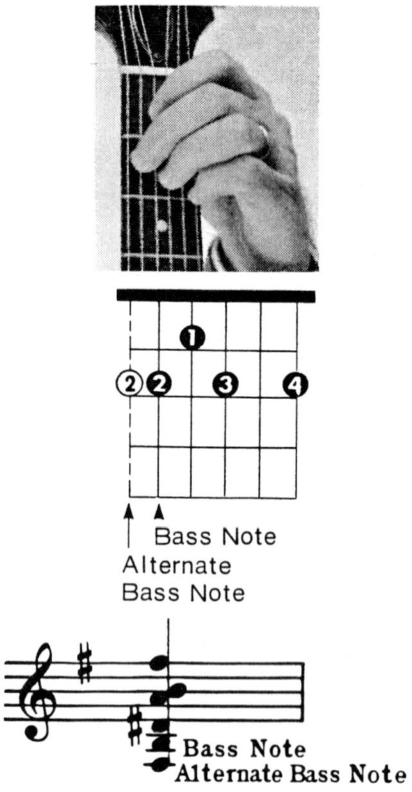

6 STRING Em CHORD

Em WITH BASS AND ALTERNATING BASS NOTE

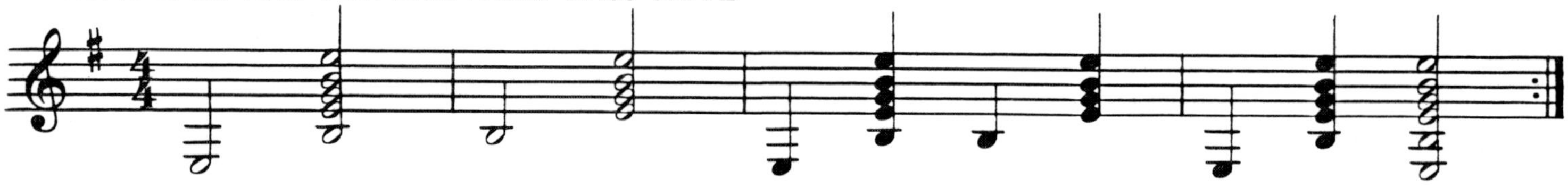

6 STRING Am CHORD

Am WITH BASS AND ALTERNATING BASS NOTE

5 STRING B7 CHORD

B7 WITH BASS AND ALTERNATING BASS NOTE

INFIRMARY BLUES

(Sing and Play)

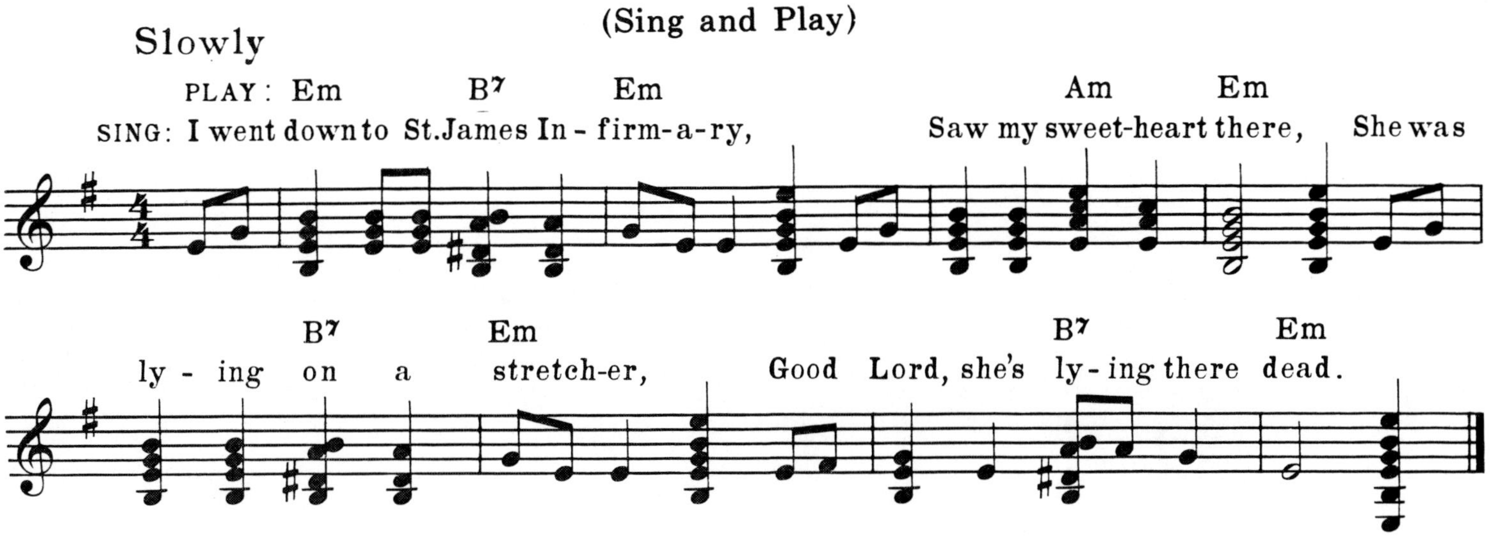
Slowly
PLAY: Em B7 Em Am Em
SING: I went down to St. James In - firm - a - ry, Saw my sweet-heart there, She was
B7 Em B7 Em
ly - ing on a stretch-er, Good Lord, she's ly - ing there dead.

LA CUMPARSITA

(Solo or Duet)

The Tango accompaniment uses the alternate bass note as the last note of every other measure. The student should learn both parts.

Moderato
SOLO
ACCOMPANIMENT
f B7
Em
1
2
B7
Em
Am
Em
B7
Em
B7 Em

THE 5 STRING C CHORD

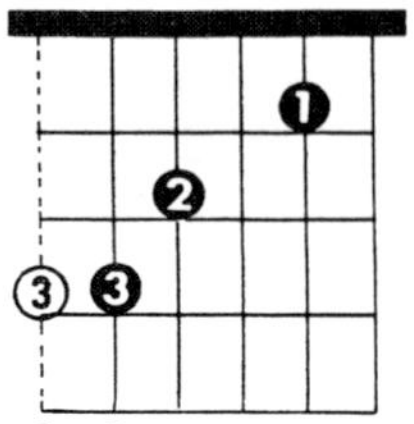

G C–Bass Note
Alternate Bass Note

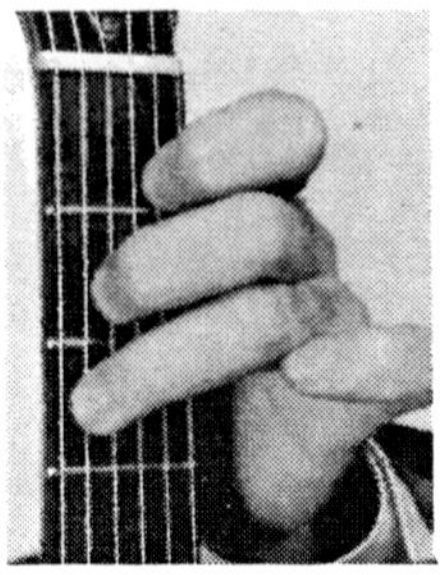

5 STRING C CHORD:

THE 4 STRING F CHORD

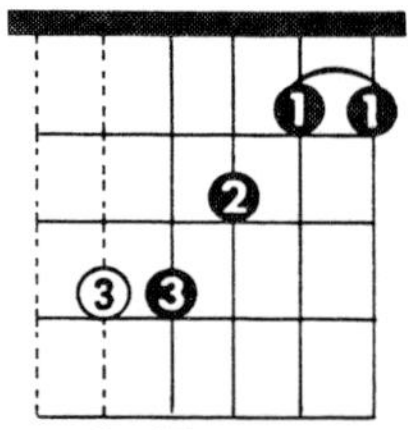

C F–Bass Note
Alternate Bass Note

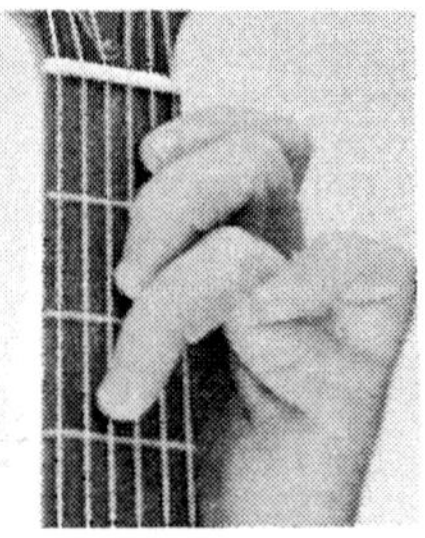

4 STRING F CHORD:

F CHORD WITH BASS NOTE:

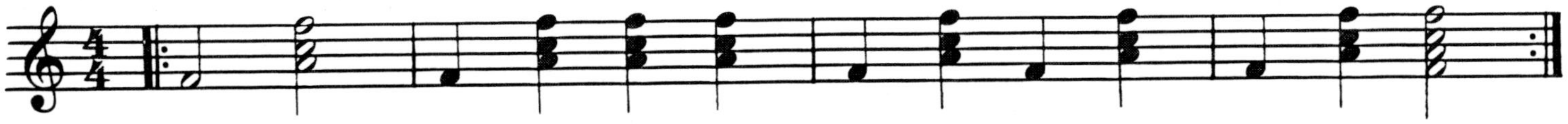

F CHORD WITH BASS AND ALTERNATE BASS:

THE 6 STRING G7 CHORD

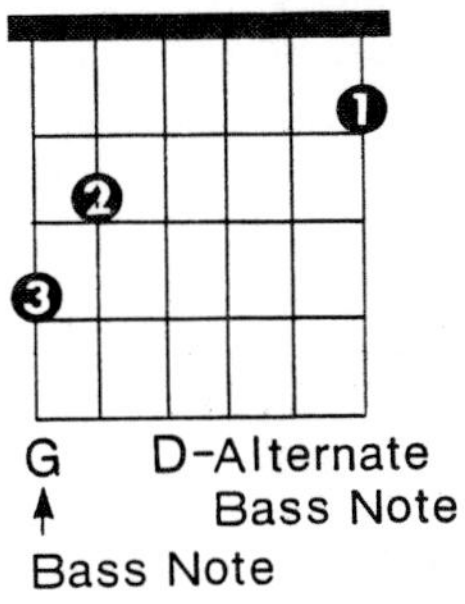

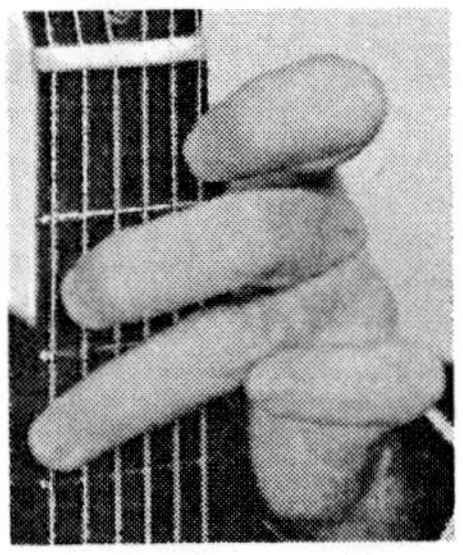

6 STRING G7 CHORD:

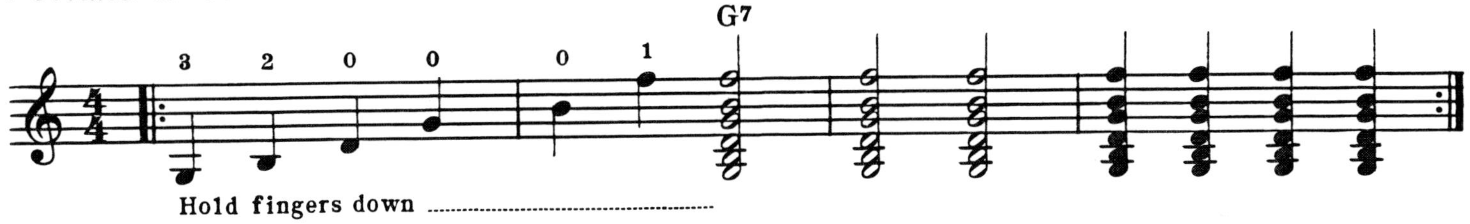

G7 CHORD WITH BASS NOTE:

G7 CHORD WITH BASS AND ALTERNATING BASS:

ACCOMPANIMENT IN C MAJOR

OUR BOYS WILL SHINE TONIGHT
(Sing and Play)

Moderato
SOLO
ACCOM-PANIMENT
C F C
f Our boys will shine to-night, Our boys will shine,
C D7 G7
We'll shine in beau - ty bright, All down the line,
C F C
Won't we look neat to-night, dressed up so fine, When the
F C F C G7 C
sun goes down, and the moon goes up, Our boys will shine.
1
2

TRIPLET STUDY

Practice two ways, slowly:

1. Using DOWN-STROKES
2. Using alternating DOWN-STROKES and UP-STROKES

WHO'S GONNA SHOE YOUR PRETTY LITTLE FOOT?

Sing and play, using alternating basses, as shown in the first line. When the 7th chord occurs for only one measure, it cannot be alternated so begin with the regular bass note.

Moderato
Who's gon-na shoe your pret - ty lit-tle foot? Who's gon-na glove your
C
F
SOLO
ACCOM-PANIMENT
mf
C
hand?
F
Who's gon-na kiss your red ru-by
C
C
lips? Who's gon-na be your man?
G7
C

FOUR WAYS TO TURN

Play four ways: (1) Play as a duet. (2) Play the 1st part as a solo. (3) Play the 2nd part as a solo. (4) Play as a longer solo by playing the 1st part through the first ending. Repeat to the beginning of the 2nd part and continue through the second ending of the 2nd part.

The chord sequence C, Am, F, G (or G7) is known as a "turn-around" in Rock 'n' Roll.

Andante
mf
gradually louder
f
mf
1.
2.
f

BASS RUNS WITHOUT CHORD CHANGES

Bass Runs are used to avoid the monotony of a continual strum or bass-chord accompaniment. They enrich the accompaniment and add an interesting variety to your playing.

Each line below is divided in two 2-measure sequences. Each 2 measures may be played repeatedly, or combined with the following sequence until the chord (the harmony) of the song changes.

When a bass run is used in a selection with alternating basses, the fundamental bass is often used first with the seventh chords.

C chord with Fundamental Bass.

// A slanting line below or following a chord symbol means to play the same chord for each line.

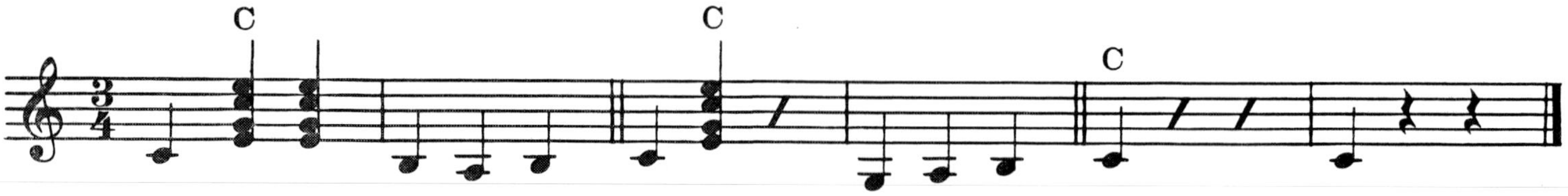

C chord with Alternating Bass

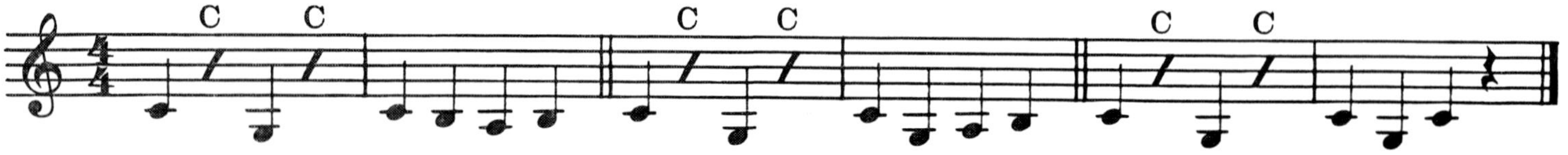

G or G7 with Fundamental Bass

G or G7 with Alternating Bass

F with Fundamental Bass

F with Alternating Bass

D7 with Fundamental Bass

D7 with Alternating and Fundamental Basses

Select several songs you have already learned and play them again, adding bass runs as shown above.

BASS RUNS WITH CHORD CHANGES

Another interesting style is to use bass runs when a chord change takes place. The runs are usually made up of the notes of the scale between the two bass notes. Some examples are shown below. From them you will get the idea of how to join any two chords more interestingly.

From C to G(7) and back to C.

In 3/4

In 4/4

From C to F and back to C.

From G(7) to C and back to G(7).

From G to D7 and back to G.

Select several songs you have already learned and add the above bass runs.

The time signature 6 ← means → six beats in each measure, 8 ← a beat on an eighth note.

Count: 1 2 3 4 5 6

Note and rest values in $\frac{6}{8}$

PADDY WHACK

Allegro

THE EYES OF TEXAS

Allegro

*D.S. is the abbreviation of Dal Segno, "The Sign."
D.S. al Fine means go back to the sign 𝄋 and play to the Fine (the end).

SIX-EIGHT ROCK
(Student-Teacher Duet)

THE KEY OF A MINOR

RELATIVE MINOR KEY OF C MAJOR

A minor and C major are relative keys. They both have the same key signature (no sharps and no flats). Like the E minor scale, the A minor scale is built on the 6th tone of the relative major, and the 7th note of the minor scale is augmented (raised a half step).

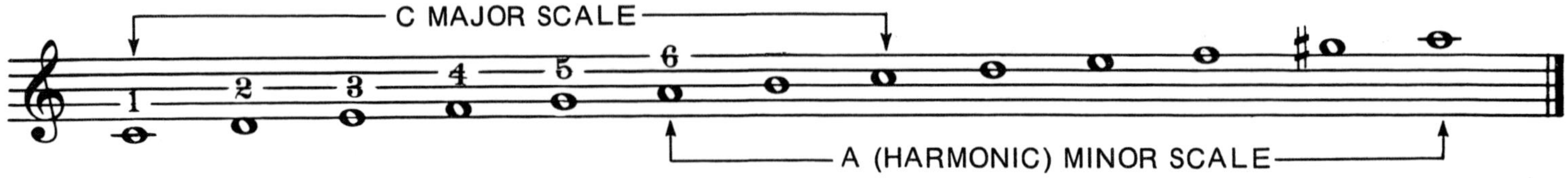

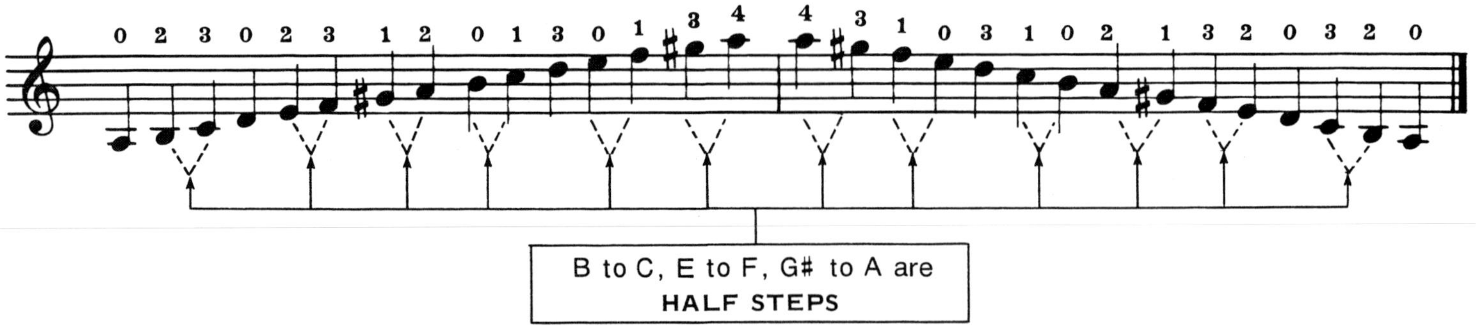

A MINOR SCALE IN CONTRARY MOTION (Duet)

THE THREE PRINCIPAL CHORDS IN A MINOR

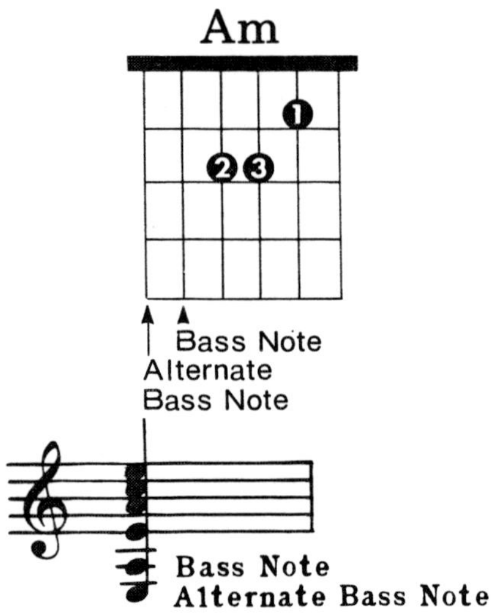

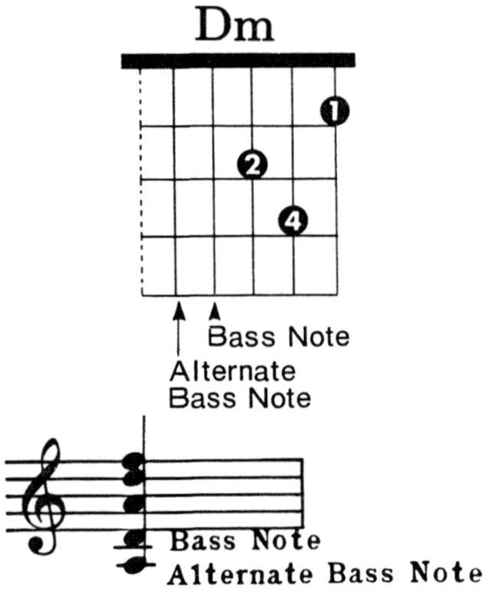

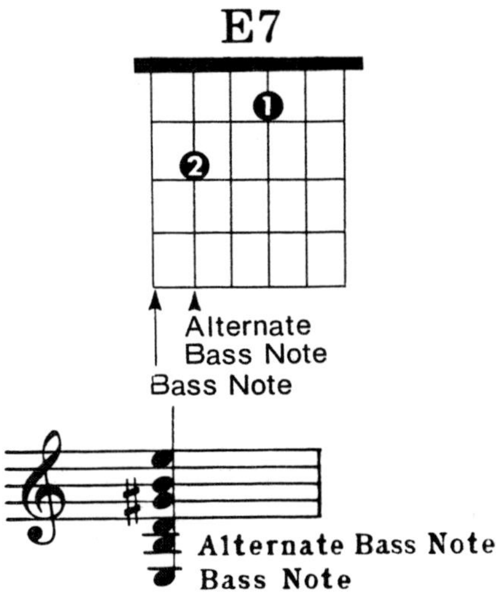

5 STRING Dm CHORD

Dm WITH BASS AND ALTERNATING BASS NOTE

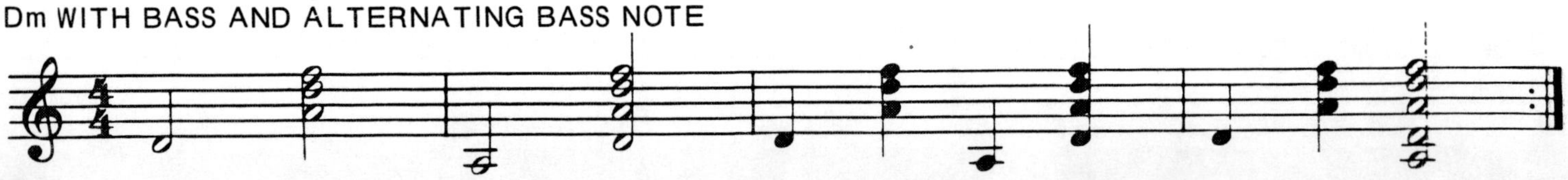

6 STRING E7 CHORD

E7 WITH BASS AND ALTERNATING BASS NOTE

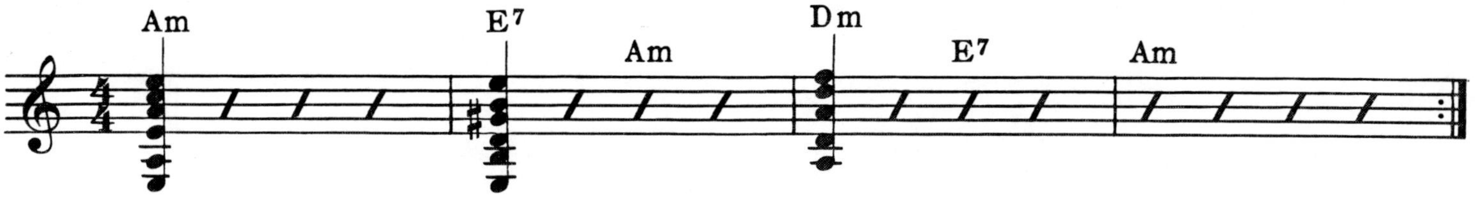

COME BACK TO SORRENTO

The teacher or student may play the accompaniment. The accompaniment should be played with bass and chord (not alternating).

Moderately slow

DANUBE WAVES

Waltz time

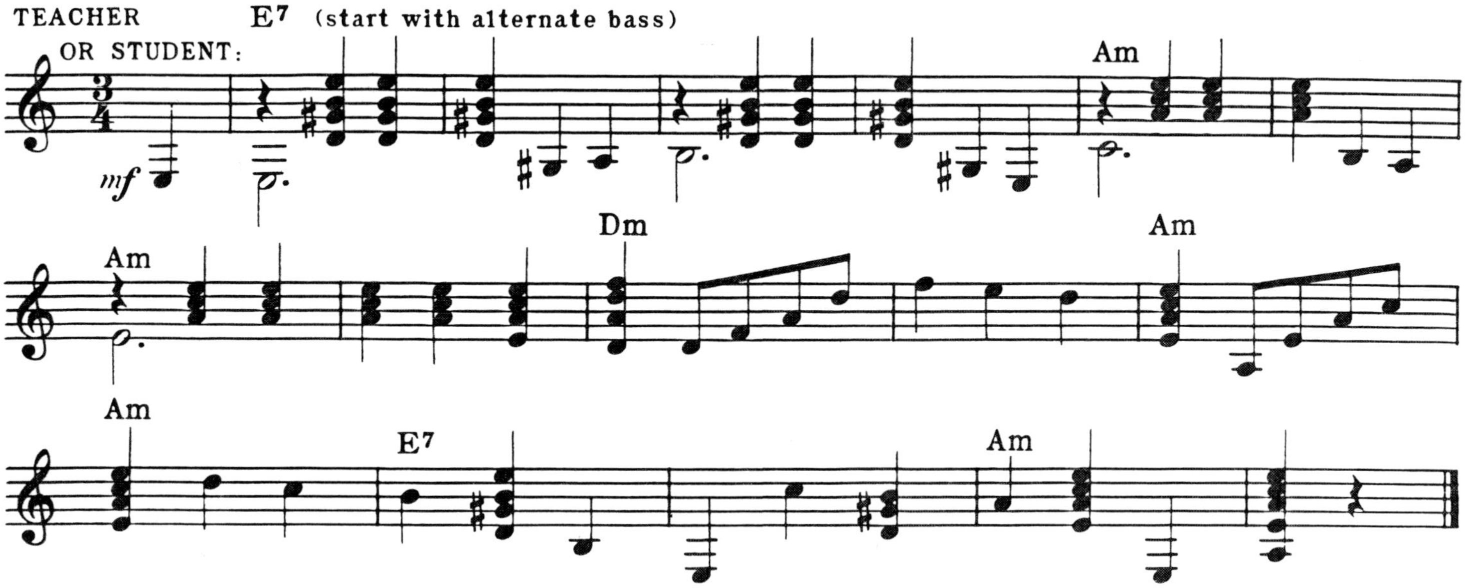

INTRODUCING THE KEY OF F MAJOR

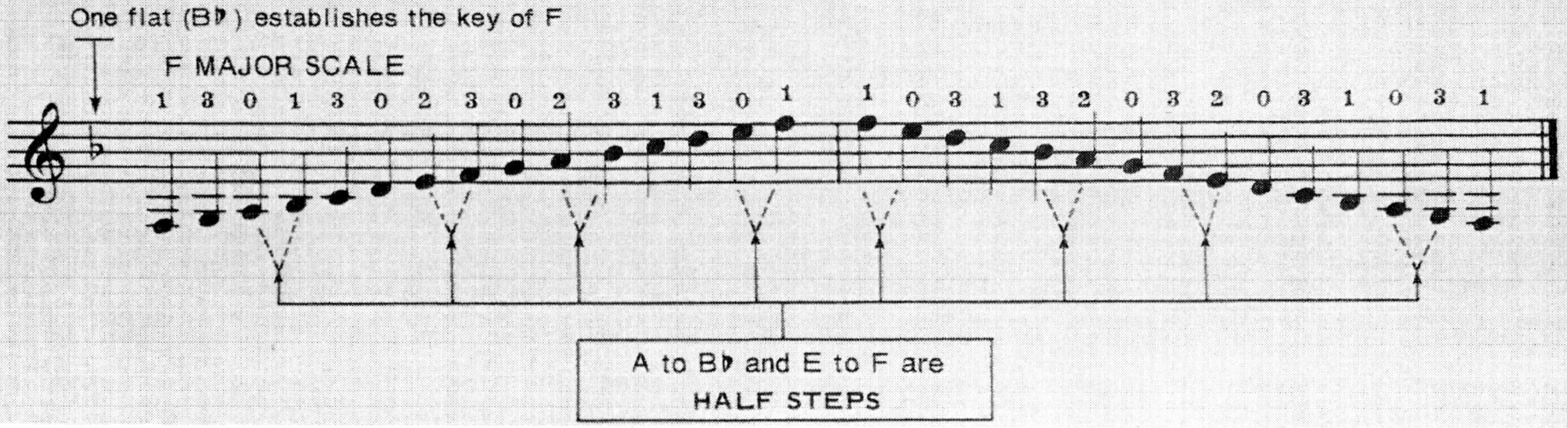

HOW TO FINGER B♭'S

F SCALE IN CONTRARY MOTION (Duet)

RAKES OF MALLOW

THE AMERICAN PATROL

*The symbol ₵ means "cut time," that is, the time value is cut in half; the half note receives 1 beat, the quarter note receives ½ beat, etc.

LO-HI ROCK

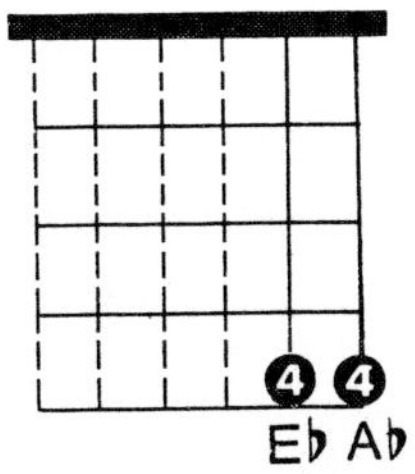

Play the high A♭ on the 1st string at the 4th fret.
Play the high E♭ on the 2nd string at the 4th fret.

Moderately fast

CHICKEN REEL

Moderato

THE THREE PRINCIPAL CHORDS IN THE KEY OF F MAJOR

THE 4 STRING F CHORD

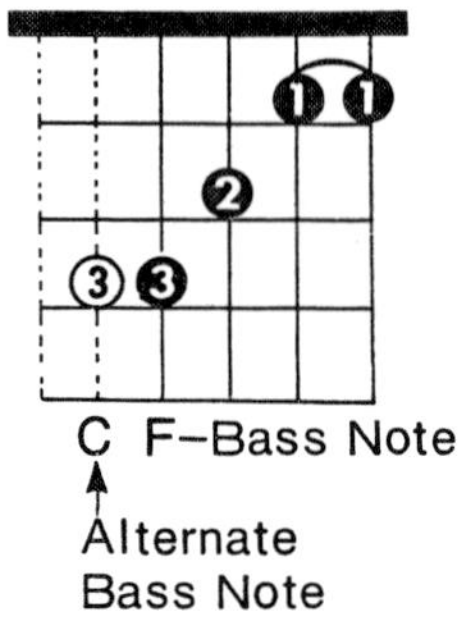

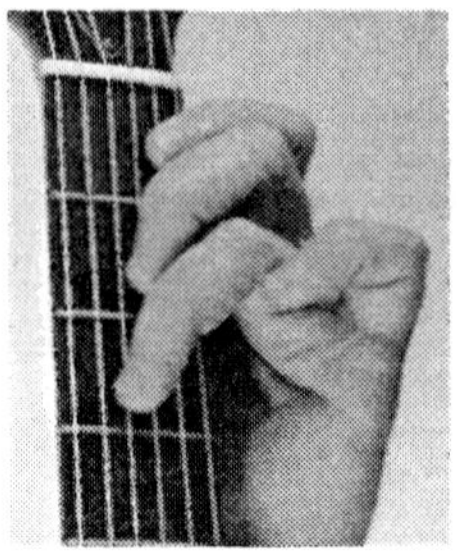

4 STRING F CHORD:

THE 4 STRING Bb CHORD

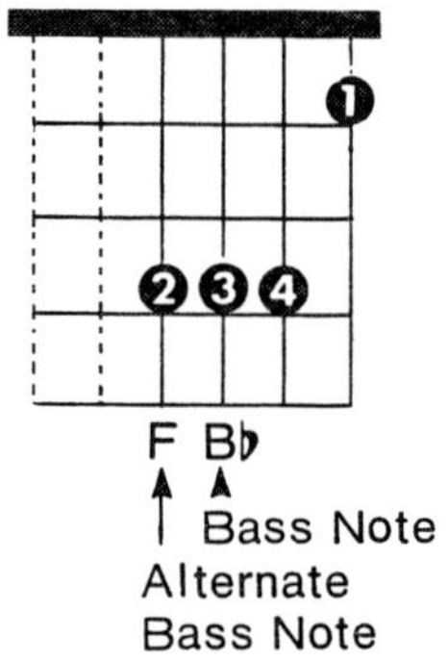

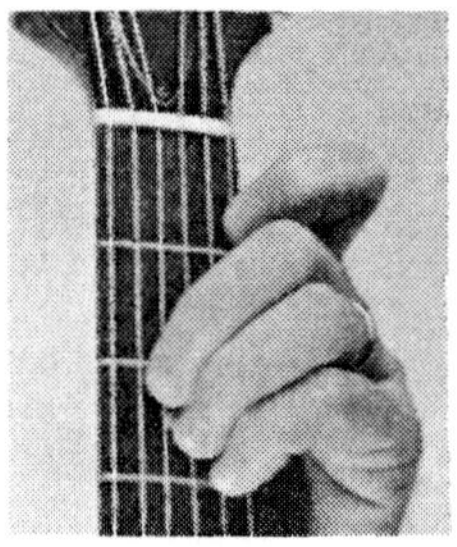

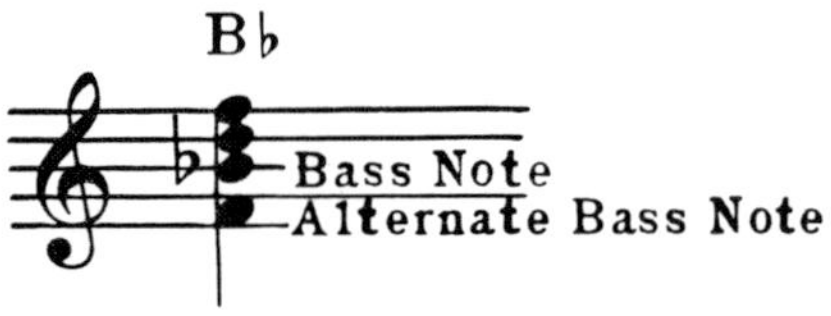

4 STRING B♭ CHORD:

B♭ CHORD WITH BASS NOTE:

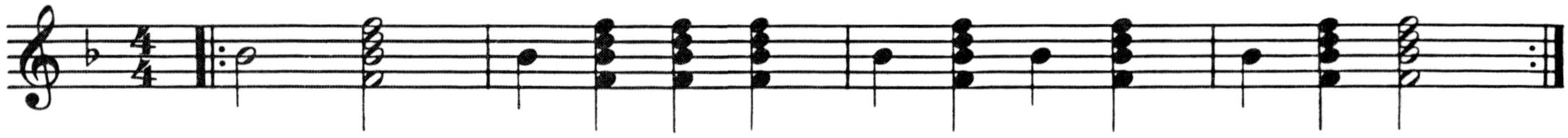

B♭ CHORD WITH BASS AND ALTERNATING BASS:

THE 5 STRING C7 CHORD

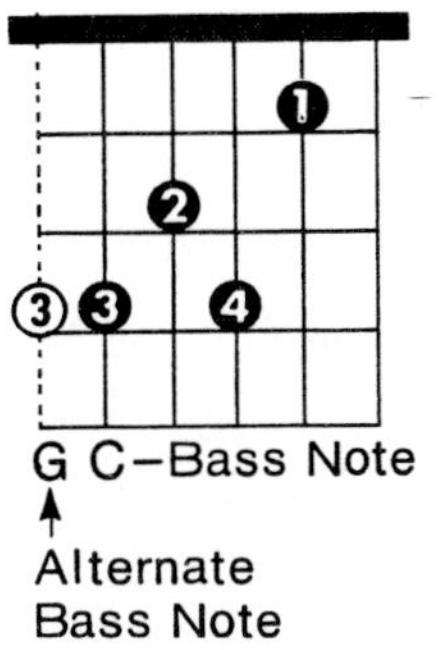

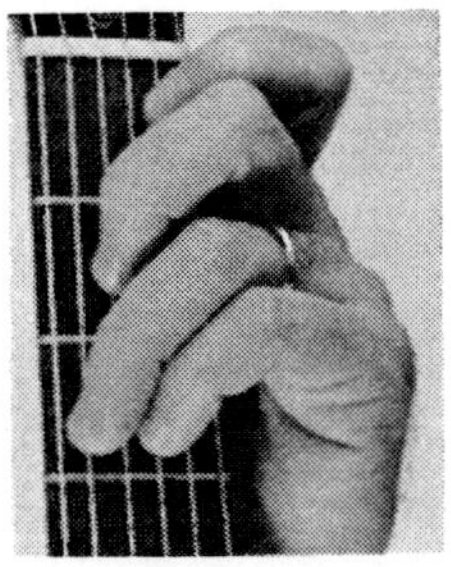

5 STRING C7 CHORD:

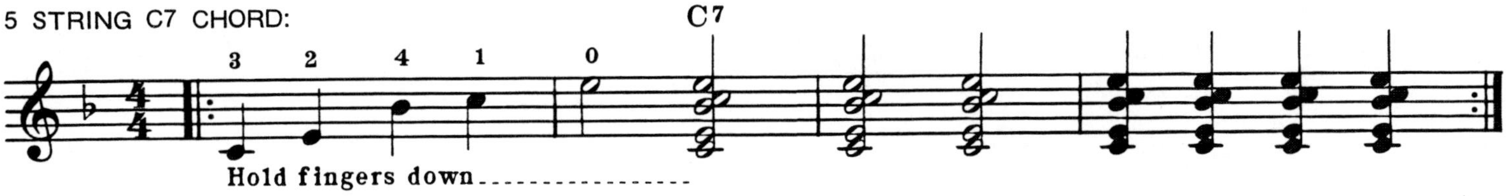

C7 CHORD WITH BASS NOTE:

C7 CHORD WITH BASS AND ALTERNATE BASS:

ACCOMPANIMENT IN F MAJOR

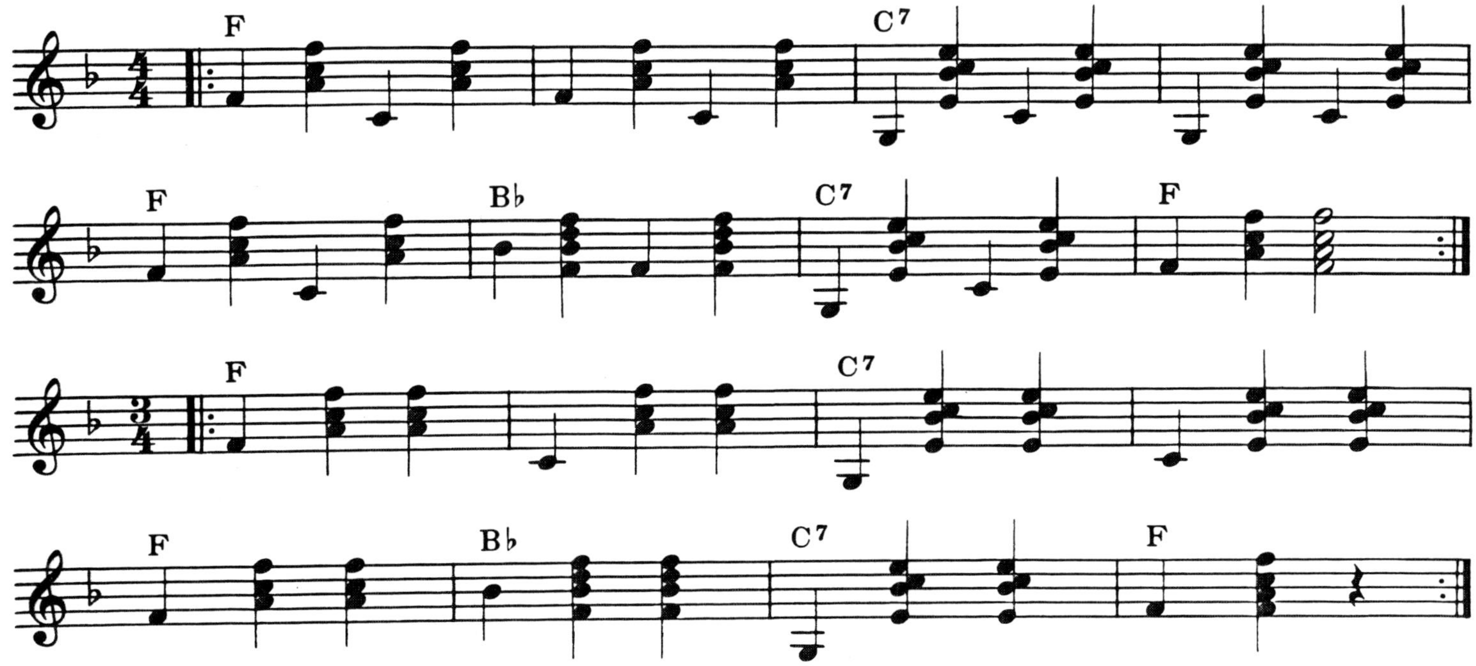

A FOR ALWAYS (Sing and Play)

Alternate the basses in the accompaniment, as shown in the first line. When the chord changes in the middle of the measure, as it does in the second measure, you will only have time to play the bass and chord.

Moderato
F Bb F C7
A for al-ways, C for care, I love a girl with gold-en hair,
SOLO
ACCOM-PANIMENT
mf
F C7 F
All the world will nev-er, nev-er know, The love I have for my la-dy-o. My
F C7 F
la-dy-o, my la-dy-o, My love-ly gold-haired la-dy-o.

CARELESS LOVE (Sing and Play-use alternating basses)

Freely
F C7 F C7
Love, oh love, oh care-less love! Love, oh love, oh care-less love!
mf
F Bb F C7 F
Love, oh love, oh care-less love! Oh, look what love has done to me!

I KNOW WHERE I'M GOING (Sing and Play-use alternating basses)

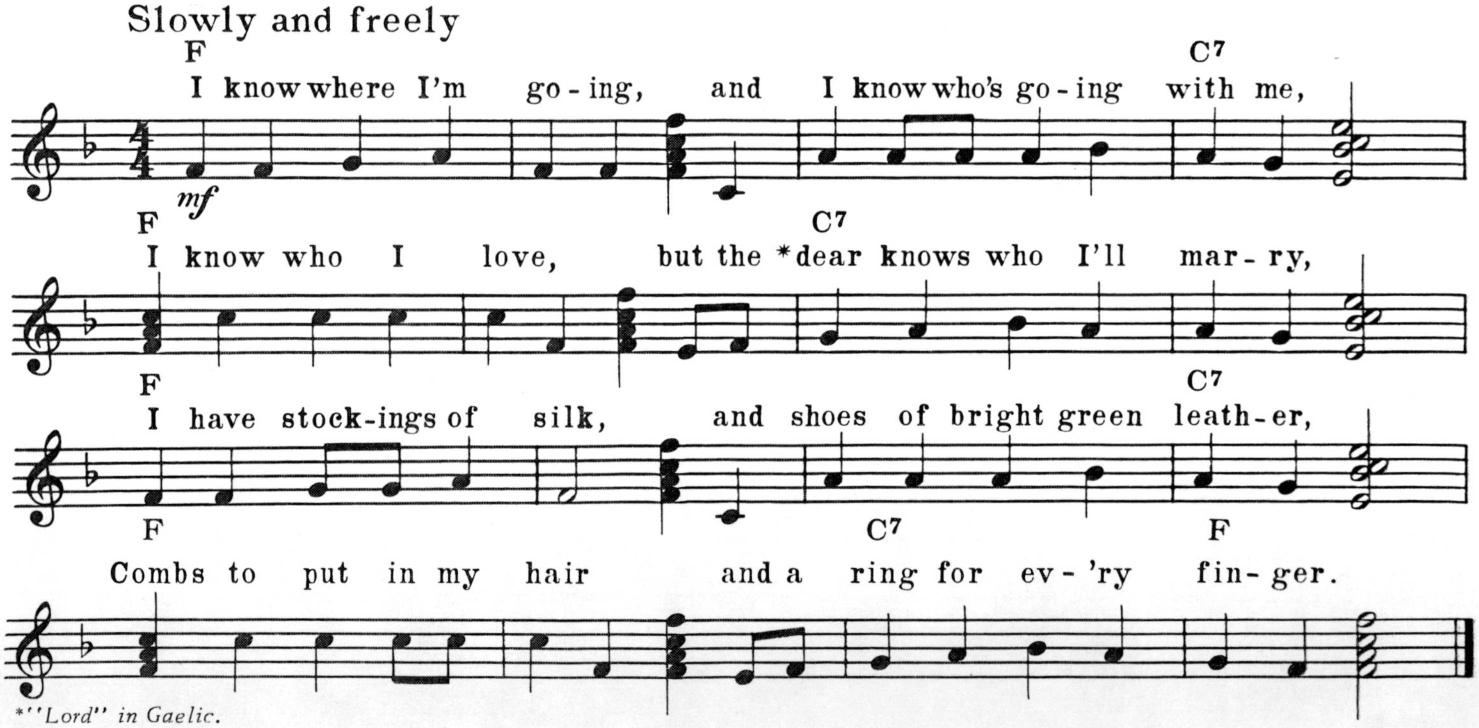
Slowly and freely
F C7
I know where I'm go-ing, and I know who's go-ing with me,
mf
F C7
I know who I love, but the *dear knows who I'll mar-ry,
F C7
I have stock-ings of silk, and shoes of bright green leath-er,
F C7 F
Combs to put in my hair and a ring for ev-'ry fin-ger.

*"Lord" in Gaelic.

TRIPLE-BEAT ROCK
(Student-Teacher Duet)

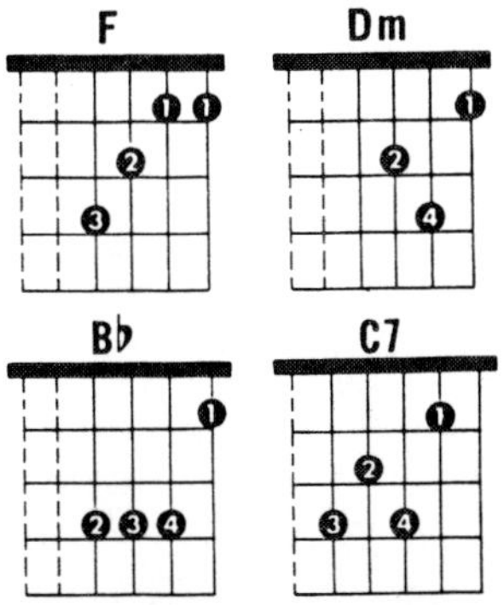

The "Turn-Around" in F uses chords in this order: F, Dm, Bb, C or C7. This selection gives excellent practice in playing F, Dm, Bb and C7 chords, which are the ones that need the most practice. It begins with 3 note chords, adding lower notes as the tune progresses. The MELODY is in the bass part, on the lower line.

Moderately slow

*  Hold each chord note as you add the next one!

THE KEY OF D MINOR

D minor is the relative minor key of F major. They both have the same key signature, one flat (B♭).

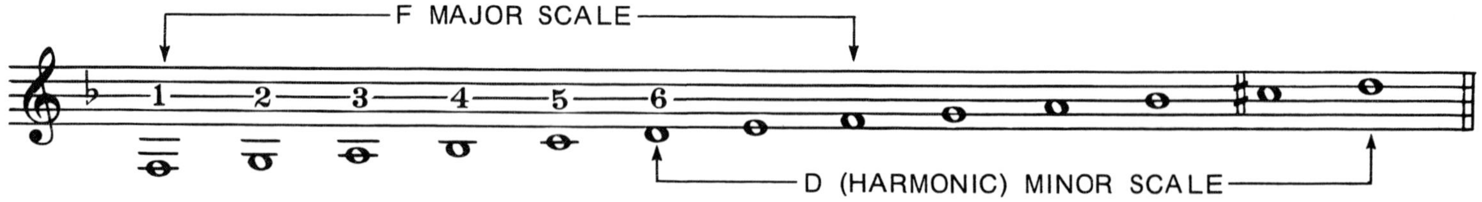

D MINOR SCALE IN CONTRARY MOTION

(Duet)

THE THREE PRINCIPAL CHORDS IN THE KEY OF D MINOR

Dm

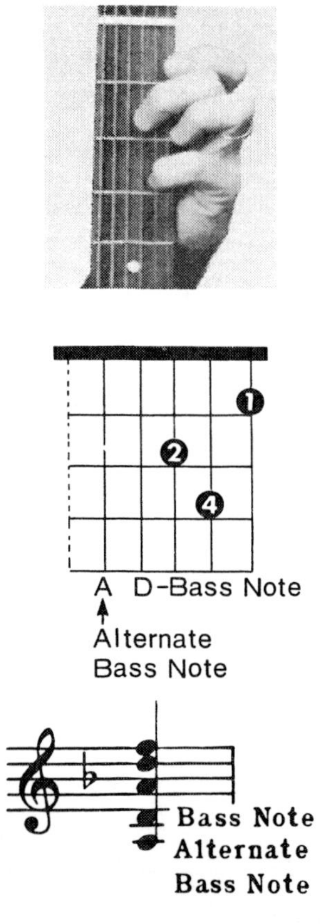

Gm

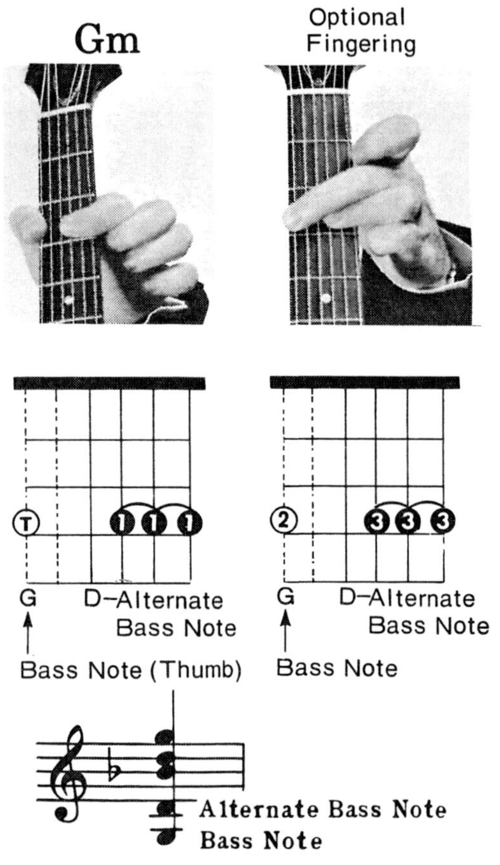

A7 (Two Forms)

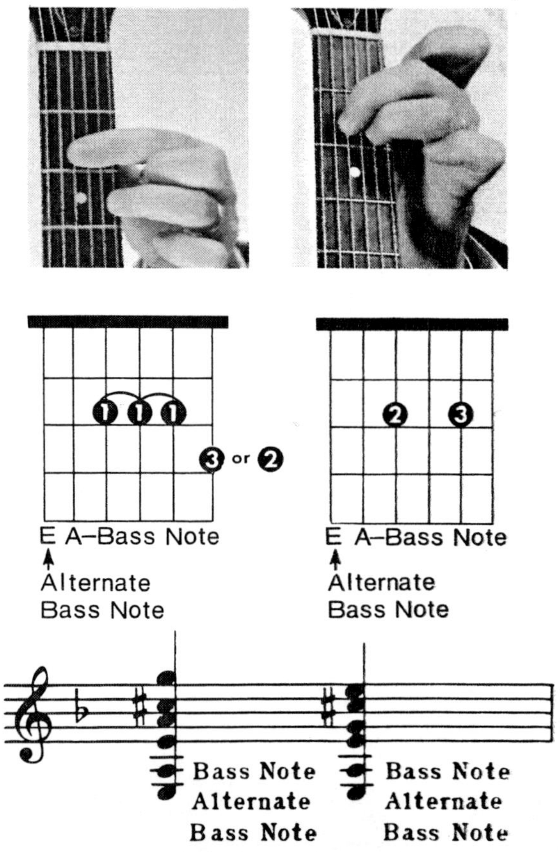

The student should learn both forms.
They are both simple and equally useful.

5 STRING Dm WITH BASS AND ALTERNATE BASS NOTE

4 STRING Gm WITH BASS AND ALTERNATE BASS NOTE

6 STRING A7 WITH BASS AND ALTERNATE BASS NOTE, FIRST FORM:

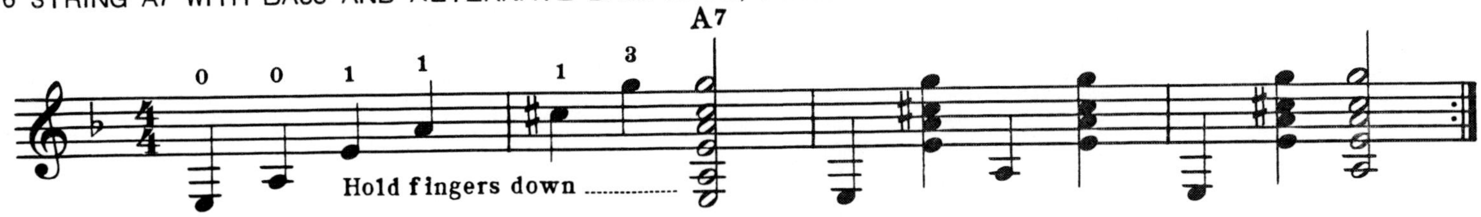

Second form:

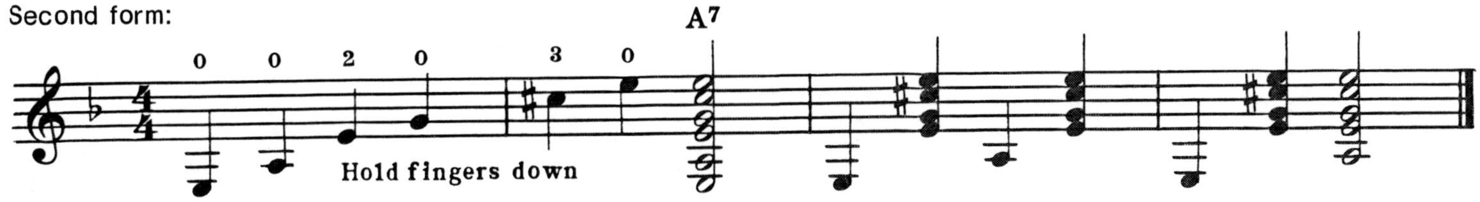

The slanting line / in the following example indicates that the previous chord is to be repeated, once for each line.

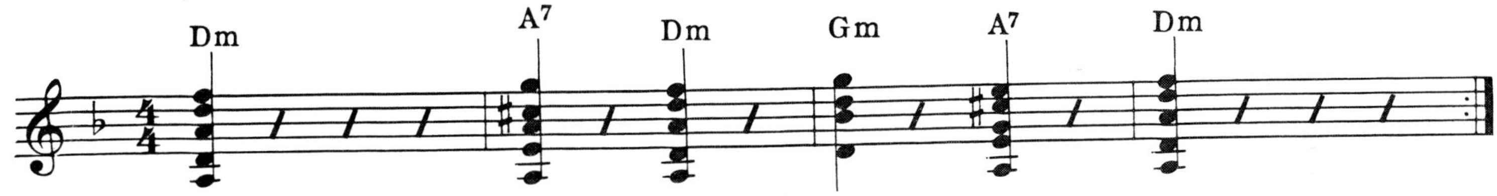

MIDNIGHT SUN
(Rock)

BATTLE OF JERICHO

Moderately fast
TEACHER OR STUDENT:
Dm A7 Dm

GO DOWN MOSES

(Duet/Sing and Play)

Andante
When Is-rael was in E-gypt's land, Let my peo-ple go! Op-
pressed so hard they could not stand, Let my peo-ple go!
Go down Mo-ses, 'Way down in E-gypt's land;
Tell old Pha-raoh, Let my peo-ple go!
Dm A7 B♭ Gm

INTRODUCING THE KEY OF D MAJOR

Two sharps (F# – C#) establishes the key of D.

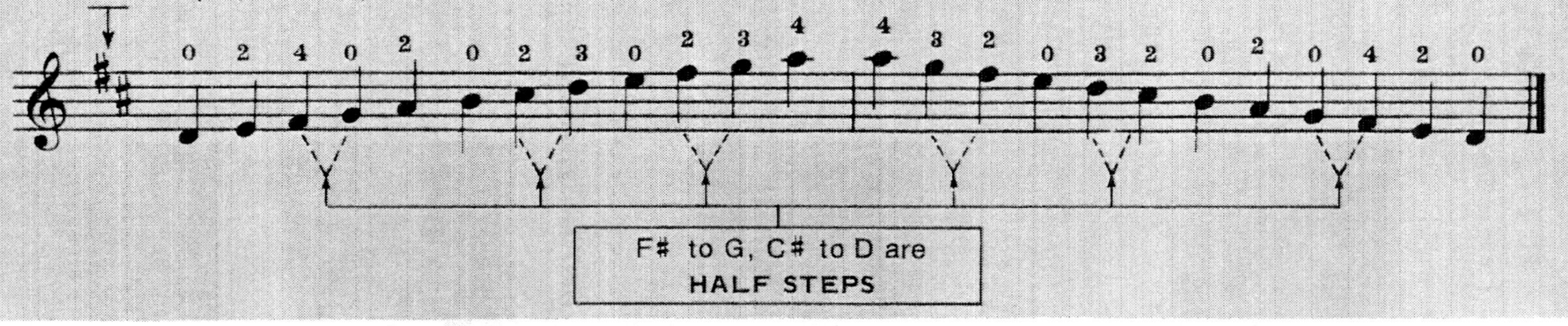

HOW TO FINGER C#'S

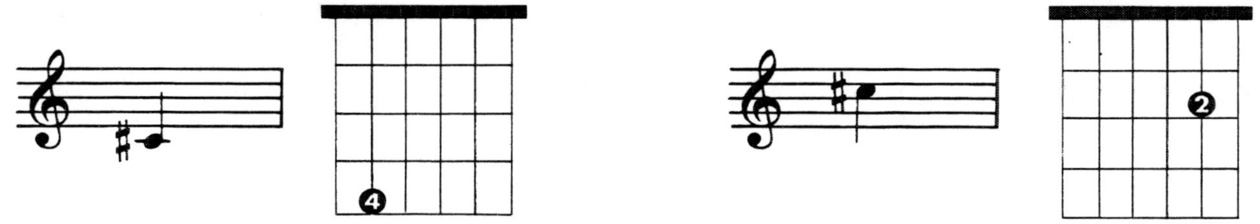

D SCALE IN CONTRARY MOTION

(Duet)

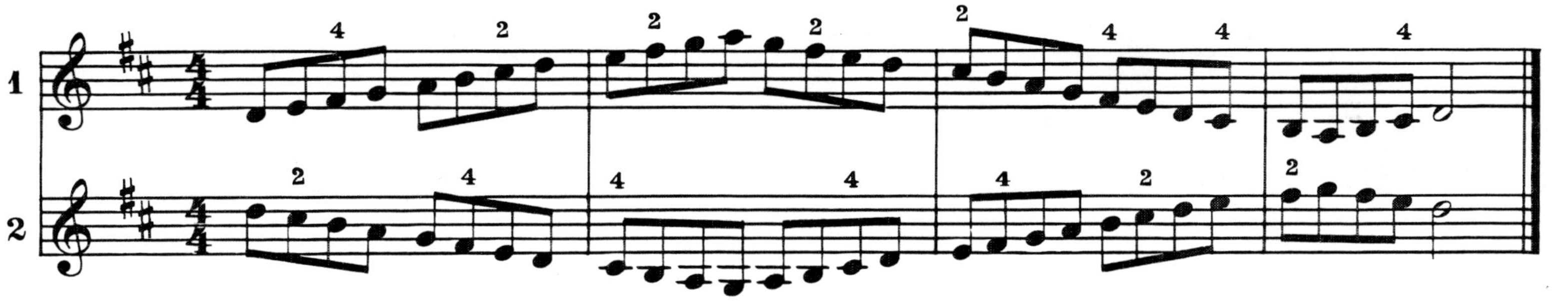

SPEED DRILL

DEVIL'S DREAM

Allegro

THE THREE PRINCIPAL CHORDS IN THE KEY OF D MAJOR

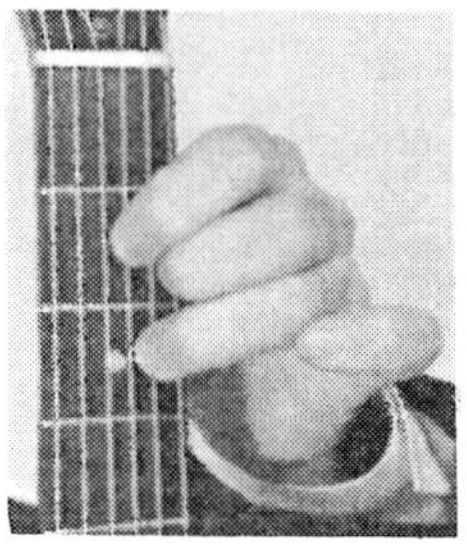

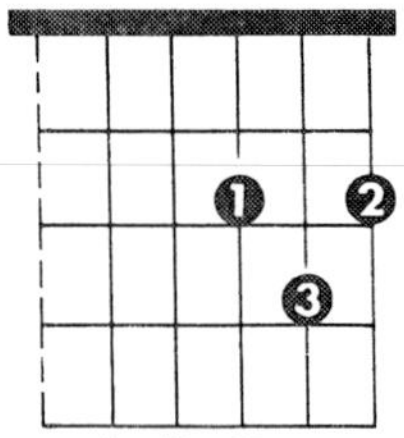

G

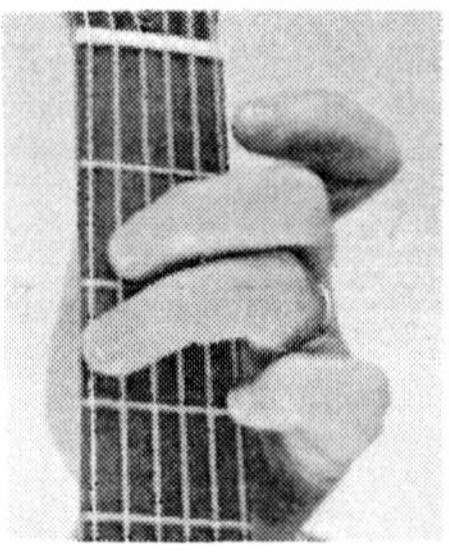

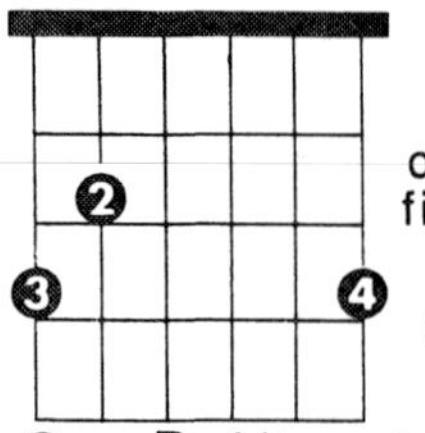

A7 (Two Forms)

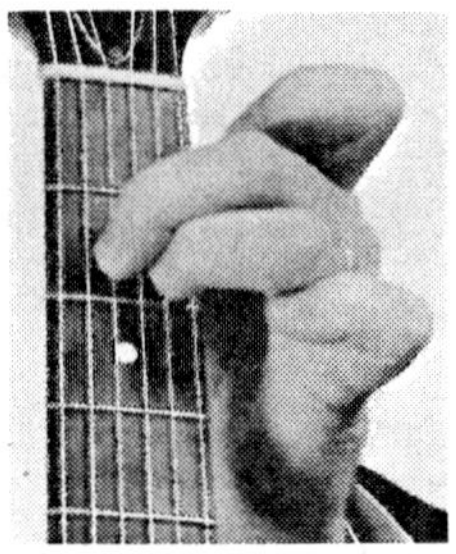

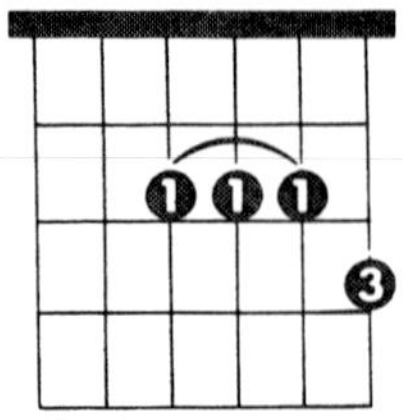

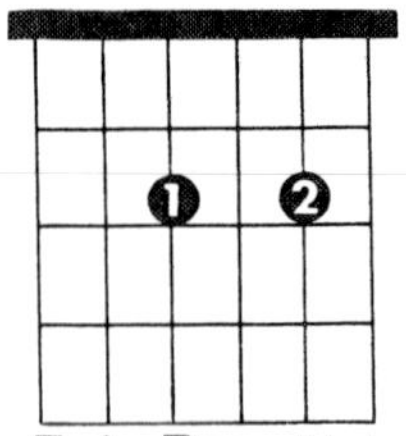

5 STRING D CHORD

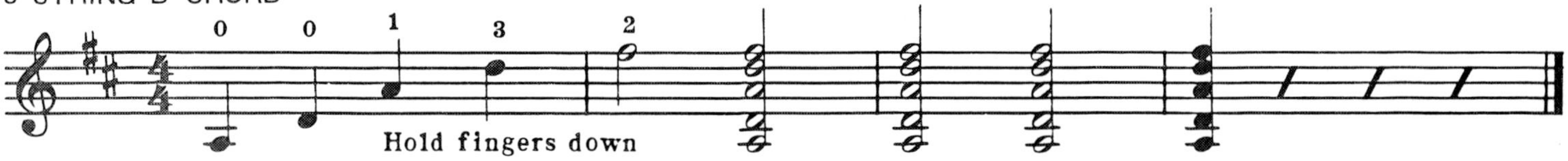

D CHORD WITH BASS NOTE

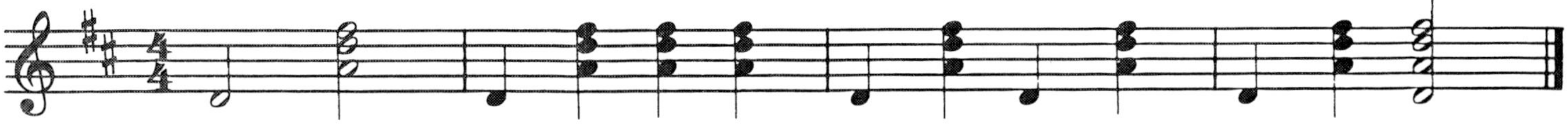

D CHORD WITH ALTERNATE BASS NOTE

6 STRING G CHORD

6 STRING A7 CHORD, first form:

Second form:

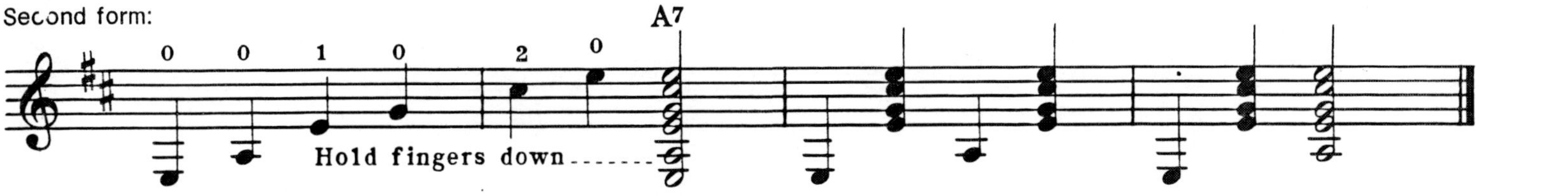

ACCOMPANIMENT IN D MAJOR

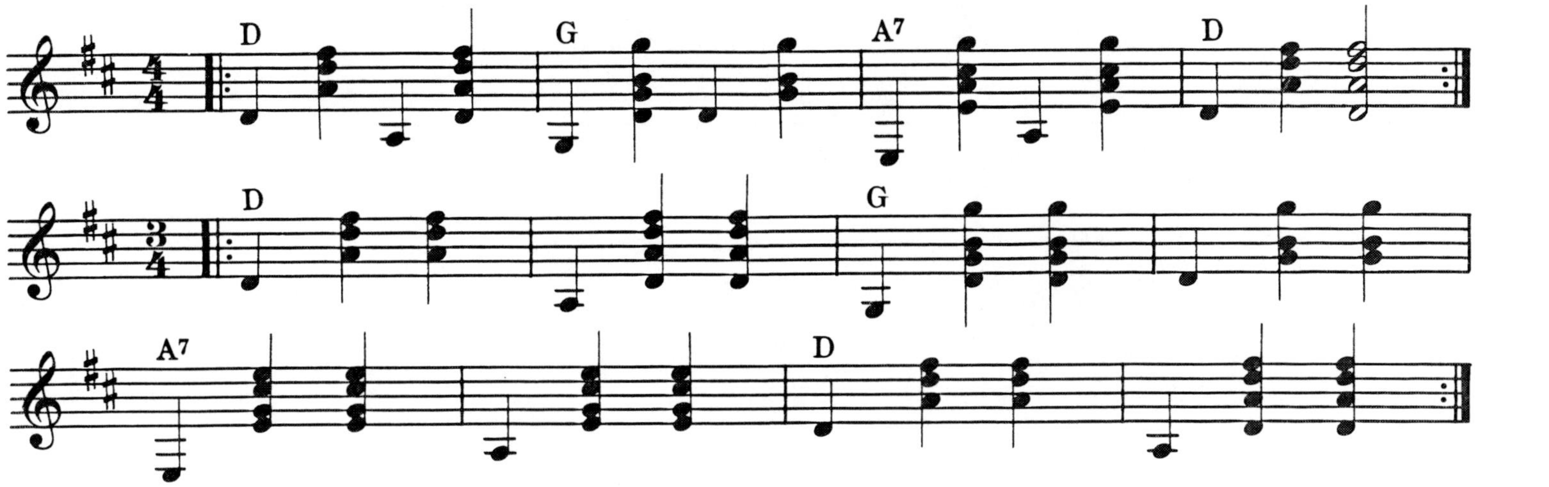

WHEN THE SAINTS GO MARCHING IN

(Sing and Play)

GREEN GROW THE LILACS

(Sing and Play)

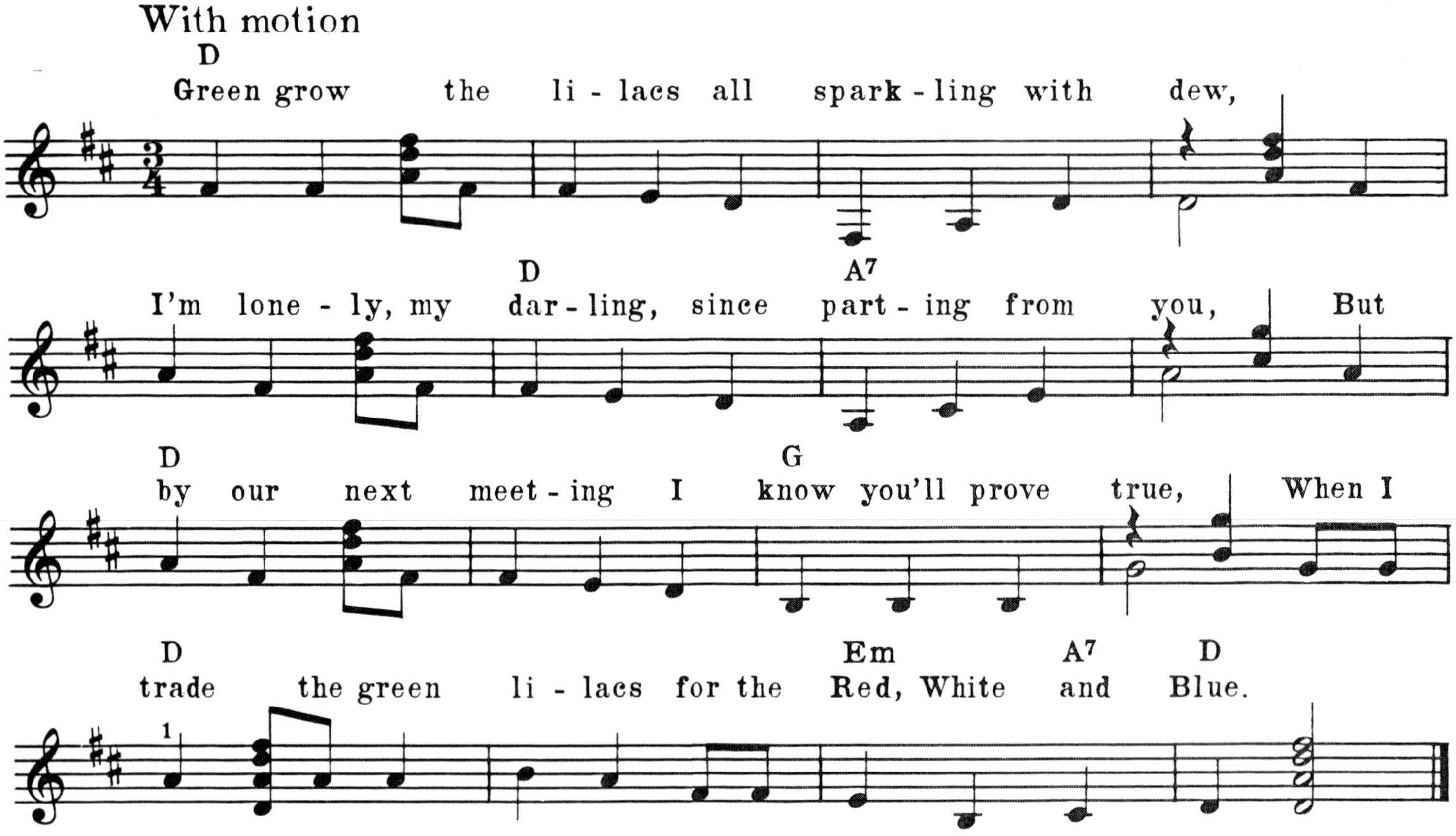
With motion
D
Green grow the li - lacs all spark - ling with dew,
D A7
I'm lone - ly, my dar - ling, since part - ing from you, But
D G
by our next meet - ing I know you'll prove true, When I
D Em A7 D
trade the green li - lacs for the Red, White and Blue.
1

EL CHOCLO

(Solo or Duet)

The student should learn both parts to this duet. The first part is complete as a solo. The second part is a more advanced form of tango rhythm and serves as an excellent chord review. Nearly every measure ends with the alternate bass of the chord in the measure that follows.

Moderately slow
1
2
f
Dm
A7
1
2
A7
Dm

1
2
Dm
D
Gm
Gm
Dm
A7
Dm
p
D
p
A7
D
B7
Em
E7
A7
f
D
f
A7
D
B7
Em
E7
A7
D

"3-D" ROCK

The student may make this selection into a duet by playing either of the following rhythms as an accompaniment:

Magic Chord Accompaniment Guide

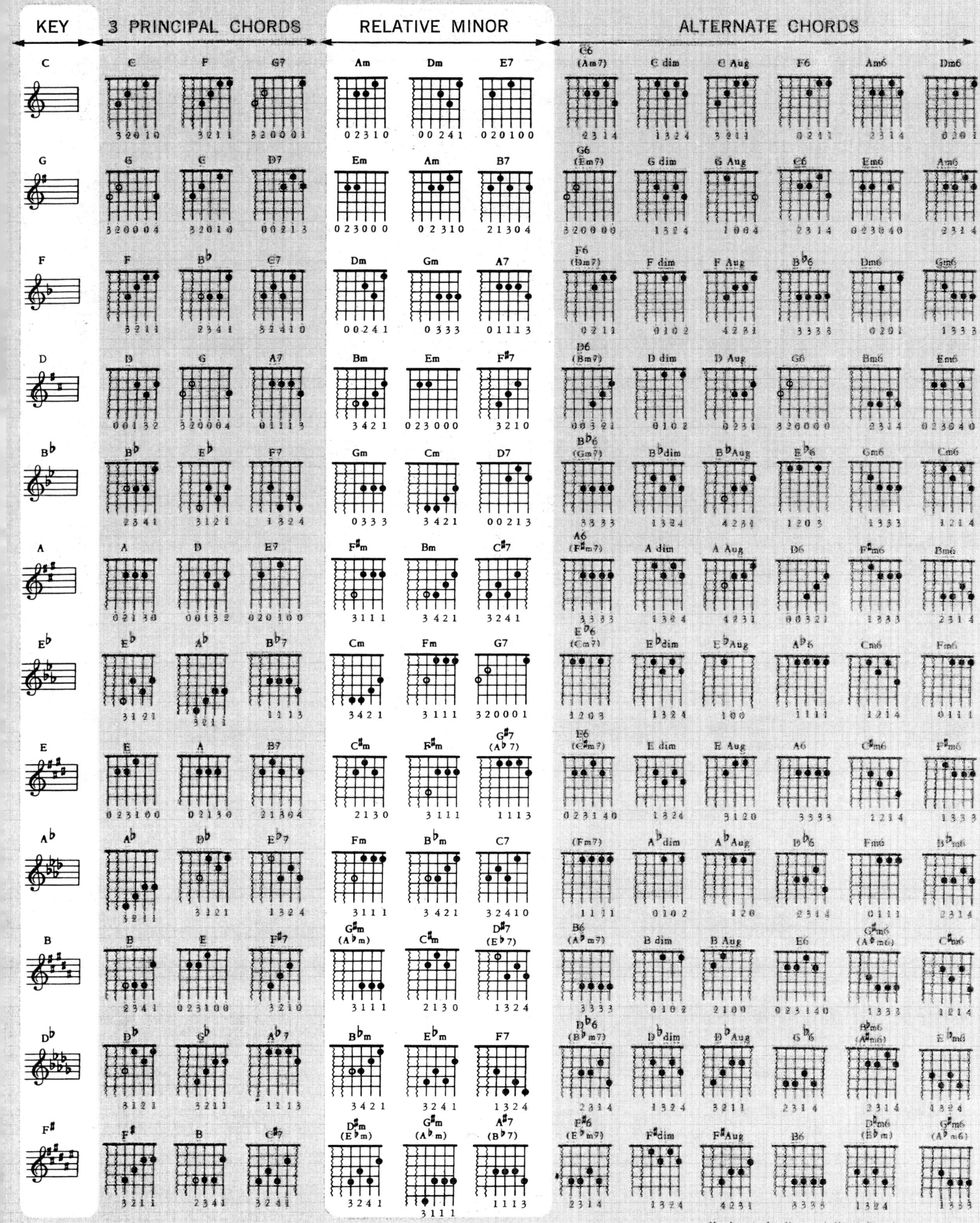

o = in chord diagram indicates optional fingering.

≀ = string not to be played.

Numbers under diagram indicate fingering:

0 = Open
1 = Index finger
2 = Middle finger
3 = Ring finger
4 = Pinky

Certificate of Promotion

This certifies that

____

has mastered and perfected

Book 2 of the New Guitar Course

and is hereby promoted into

Book 3 of the New Guitar Course

or Book 3 of Alfred's Basic Guitar Method

TEACHER ______________________________

DATE ____________________